REAL CITY

Barcelona

REAL CITY

Barcelona

www.realcity.dk.com

LONDON, NEW YORK,
MELBOURNE, MUNICH AND DELHI
www.dk.com

Contributors
Daniel Campi, Sally Davies, Kirsten Foster, Mary-Ann Gallagher, Tara Stevens

Photographers
Alessandro Santarelli, Susannah Sayler

Reproduced in Singapore by Colourscan
Printed and bound in Singapore by Tien Wah Press

First American Edition, 2007
07 08 09 10 9 8 7 6 5 4 3 2 1

Published in the United States by
DK Publishing, Inc.,
375 Hudson Street, New York, New York 10014

ISSN: 1933-4567
ISBN: 978-0-75662-683-9

The information in this Real City guide is checked annually.

This guide is supported by a dedicated website which provides the very latest information for visitors
to Barcelona; please see page 7 for the web address and password. Some information, however, is
liable to change, and the publishers cannot accept responsibility for any consequences arising from
the use of this book, nor for any material on third party websites, and cannot guarantee that any
website address in this book will be a suitable source of travel information.
We value the views and suggestions of our readers very highly. Please write to:
Publisher, DK Eyewitness Travel Guides,
Dorling Kindersley, 80 Strand, London WC2R 0RL, Great Britain.

Contents

The Guide

Real City Barcelona

Stay ahead of the crowd with **Real City Barcelona**, and find the best places to eat, shop, drink and chill out at a glance.

The guide is divided into four main sections:

Introducing Barcelona – essential background information on the city, including an overview by one of the authors, the top tourist attractions, festivals and seasonal events, and useful travel and practical information.

Listings – eight themed chapters packed with incisive reviews of the best the city has to offer, in every price band and chosen by local experts.

Street Finder – map references in the listings lead you to this section, where you can plan your route and find your way around.

Indexes – the By Area and By Type indexes offer shortcuts to what you are looking for, whether it is a bar in the Old City or a seafood restaurant.

The Website

www.realcity.dk.com

By purchasing this book you have been granted free access to up-to-the-minute online content about Barcelona for at least 12 months. Click onto **www.realcity.dk.com** for updates, and sign up for a free weekly email with the latest information on what to see and do in Barcelona.

On the website you can:

- **Find the latest news** about Barcelona, including exhibitions, restaurant openings and music events

- Check what other readers have to say and **add your own comments** and reviews

- **Plan your visit** with a customizable calendar

- See at a glance **what's in and what's not**

- Look up listings by name, by type and by area, and check the **latest reviews**

- **Link directly** to all the websites in the book, and many more

How to register

❯ Click on the Barcelona icon on the home page of the website to register or log in.

❯ Enter the city code given on this page, and follow the instructions given.

❯ The city code will be valid for a minimum of 12 months from the date you purchased this guide.

city code: **barcelona31854**

introducing barcelona

One of the world's most stylish cities, Barcelona is full of amazing architecture, design and artworks. It is also home to some of the most exciting restaurants, thanks to a strong culinary tradition and the inventive Catalan spirit. This guide leads you to Barcelona's latest and best, starting with its most popular sights and year-round festivities.

INTRODUCING BARCELONA

The view of Barcelona from the top of Montjuïc reveals what I think is Barcelona's greatest charm – its human scale. While the Catalan capital is large enough to offer all the big-city thrills, it's also small enough to explore on foot – the time capsule of the Gothic Quarter being particularly good for an aimless amble. Barcelona is no museum city, however, and the streets and squares hum night and day, offering unlimited options for shopping, dining and nightlife.

Mary-Ann Gallagher

Mediterranean Barcelona

Curled languidly around the shores of the Mediterranean, Barcelona is happily blessed with year-round sunshine. Life is lived outdoors to a great extent: families gather on café-trimmed squares, the elderly cluster on benches to gossip, and fashion victims walk their designer dogs past the chic boutiques of the Passeig del Born *(see p132)*. At the heart of every neighbourhood is a market. The most celebrated is the Boqueria on Las Ramblas *(see pp13 & 131)*, where besides traditional favourites like pigs' trotters you'll find chocolate-dipped scorpions and pungent exotic fruit. More down-to-earth is the Mercat Sant Antoni *(see p66)*, a pretty Modernista market surrounded by excellent local produce shops. The fashion pack flock to the new Mercat de Santa Caterina *(see p132)*, stunningly capped with an undulating roof of multi-coloured tiles. In summer, the city's inhabitants flee to the hills or the beaches. By day, every inch of sand is covered with a mix of local families and tourists, while glossy young Barcelonins hang out at the string of beach bars when the sun goes down.

The locals are laid-back and deliberate, serene in their belief that everything will happen in its own time. Their pace, as they amble past the flower stalls dotting Las Ramblas or pause to consider a consignment of ripe melons in the market, is unhurried and relaxed, echoing the rhythms of the Mediterranean.

Catalan Capital

Barcelona is the proud capital of an ancient nation with its own distinctive culture, language and traditions. The most obvious sign of difference is the language: street signs, menus, metro tickets, bus timetables and shop opening hours are all posted in Catalan, which has enjoyed a resurgence since the years of repression under Franco. Festivals are an important part of the culture, and during the city's excellent festivals, *capgrossos* (fatheads) and *gegants* (giants) parade through the streets. The most thrilling local tradition, however, is the *correfoc* (fire-running), when dragons and demons race through the streets spitting fire at the shrieking crowds. Every neighbourhood has its own

a city primer

festival. Gràcia's *(see p17)* is the most atmospheric, but the fabulous week-long *Festes de la Mercè (see p18)* at the end of September is the biggest and best.

Modernista Barcelona

Barcelona is the home of Modernista architecture, and the style's visionary architects created a splendid array of buildings in the Eixample, the 19th-century extension of the city. Essential to the credo of Modernisme (a movement very much distinct from Modernism) was the notion that everything was worthy of fine crafts-manship. While Gaudí, Montaner and Cadafalch may be the acknowledged masters of the style *(see pp76 & 89)*, also look out for the work of lesser-known architects, especially along the Rambla de Catalunya. Don't miss Farmàcia Bolós at No. 77, or Casa Dolors Calm at No. 54.

Contemporary City

The city's skyline reveals a long-standing obsession with all that's new and different, particularly in such striking contemporary buildings as the Mercat de Santa Caterina and the Torre Agbar at Plaça de les Glories in Poblenou. Experimentation and innovation are key elements of Barcelona's psyche, and in its performing arts the city really excels at cutting-edge contemporary dance and drama, such as that staged at the Teatre Lliure *(see p99)* and Mercat de les Flors *(see p100)*. The same commitment to innovation can be found in Barcelona's kitchens, where a whole new generation of chefs has emerged, inspired by Catalan giants such as Ferran Adrià, Carme Ruscalleda and Santi Santamaría. As for fashion, take a stroll down Carrer d'Avinyó *(see p53)* or the little alleys spidering off Passeig del Born *(see p132)* to find boutiques stacked with the quirky styles that characterize the city's fashion.

✅ The Good Value Mark

Cities can be expensive, but if you know where to go you can always discover excellent-value places. We've picked out the best of these in the Restaurants, Shopping and Hotels chapters and indicated them with the pink Good Value mark.

INTRODUCING BARCELONA

Throughout the main chapters of this guide, we take you under the surface of the city, to tucked away bars, the hippest clubs, the best restaurants and the most dependable venues for live events. But such well-known and emblematic sights as the Sagrada Família and La Pedrera, and such popular destinations as Las Ramblas and the Fundació Joan Miró are loved by both visitors and locals alike. They number among Barcelona's most unmissable sights.

Sagrada Família
`2 H4`

C/Mallorca 401 • 93 207 30 31 • Sagrada Família metro
>> www.sagradafamilia.org Open 9am–8pm daily (to 6pm Oct–Mar)

Gaudí's great church – and Barcelona's most exuberant symbol – remains unfinished, more than 80 years after the architect's death. However, work continues and the current aim is to complete it by 2026, the anniversary of Gaudí's death *(see p76)*. **Adm**

Casa Batlló
`2 E5`

Passeig de Gràcia 43 • 93 216 0306 • Passeig de Gràcia metro
>> www.casabatllo.es Open 9am–8pm daily

Gaudí's delirious imprint is everywhere in Barcelona. This magnificent mansion shimmers with scaly tiles, while inside ceilings swirl like Italian ice cream, the staircase makes a flamboyant swoop and balconies are formed by sinuous tendrils *(see p76)*. **Adm**

La Pedrera (Casa Milà)
`2 E4`

C/Provença 261–5 • 902 400 973 • Diagonal 28 metro
>> www.lapedreraeducacio.org Open 10am–8pm daily

There isn't a straight line anywhere in Gaudí's extraordinary apartment building: even the door handles undulate, echoing the curving walls and windows. Practical features, such as air vents on the roof, are cleverly turned into surreal sculptures, and the overall effect produces one of the most striking sights in Barcelona *(see p76)*. **Adm**

For the very latest on Barcelona go to >> **www.realcity.dk.com**

top attractions

Park Güell

C/Olot • 93 213 0488 • Lesseps metro
Open 10am–dusk

Barcelona's most celebrated park sprawls across a hilltop, offering breathtaking views across the city and out to sea. It was designed by Gaudí and his patron Eusebi Güell (after whom it is named), and at its heart is the modest pink villa which was Gaudí's home *(see p76)*.

Las Ramblas

5 C2

Drassanes, Liceu or Catalunya metro
La Boqueria market open 8am–8:30pm Mon–Sat (several stalls close much earlier)

The city's showcase promenade, Las Ramblas is actually five streets placed end-to-end, each with its own personality. Barcelona's legendary Boqueria market is piled high with fresh produce, and its counter bars offer some of the city's best snacks and coffee *(see p131)*.

Catedral de Barcelona

6 E3

Plaça de la Seu • 93 315 1554 • Jaume I metro
>> www.catedralbcn.org Open 8am–12:45pm & 5:15pm–7:30pm daily

The theatrical spiky façade of Barcelona's Gothic cathedral dominates the Old City. At its heart is the palm-shaded cloister, where white geese dwell and Barcelona's former merchants and guild members are buried. Inside the church is the operatic white marble tomb of the city's patron saint, Saint Eulàlia *(see p79)*.

>> *Take the lift to the rooftop of the cathedral for fabulous views of the city*

INTRODUCING BARCELONA

MNAC

3 A2

Parc de Montjuïc • 93 622 0360 • Espanya metro
>> www.mnac.es Open 10am–7pm Tue–Sat, 10am–2:30pm Sun

Highlights of this museum devoted to Catalan art include frescoes
from Romanesque churches high in the Pyrenees, Gothic paintings
shimmering with gold and the fabulous Thyssen Collection, which
includes works by Fra Angelico, Titian and Velázquez *(see p86)*.

Fundació Joan Miró

3 B3

Parc de Montjuïc • 93 443 9470 • Espanya metro then bus 50 or 55
>> www.bcn.fjmiro.es Open 10am–8pm Tue–Sat (Oct–Jun to 7), 10–2:30 Sun

A stunning white building drenched with light is home to this
excellent museum dedicated to the prolific Catalan artist Joan Miró.
It contains a vast collection of his output in all media, stretching
from early paintings to his final works *(see p87)*.

Museu Picasso

6 F3

C/Montcada 15–23 • 93 319 6310 • Jaume I metro
>> www.museupicasso.bcn.es Open 10am–8pm Tue–Sun

Five medieval palaces were converted to house Barcelona's most
visited museum, which contains a huge collection of Picasso's works.
Among the finest paintings are those from his Blue Period – haunting
figures modelled on prostitutes and Gypsies – though the highlight is
his meditation on Velázquez's masterpiece *Las Meninas (see p81)*.

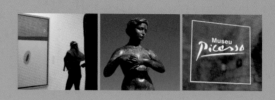

top attractions

Palau de la Música Catalana

6 F1

C/Sant Francesc de Paula 2 • 90 244 2882 • Urqinaona metro
>> www.palaumusica.org Guided visits 10am–3:30pm daily

Domènech i Montaner's Palau de la Música erupts like an exploding bouquet from the corner of a dusty old street. The interior is equally overwhelming, with rainbow-coloured light streaming into the auditorium through a stained-glass skylight *(see p98)*.

Montjuïc

3 B4

Paral.lel metro, then funicular, then cable-car

Barcelona's favourite playground, Montjuïc juts over the sea south of the Old City. Leafy parks and gardens provide a cool retreat, and the views from the fortress at the top are exceptional. Other attractions include the enjoyably kitsch model village, Poble Espanyol (www. poble-espanyol.com) , and outdoor film screenings in summer.

Tibidabo

Tram from Avinguda del Tibidabo then funicular, or Tibibús from Plaça Catalunya
>> www.tibidabo.es

Behind the city looms the fun-filled hill of Tibidabo. Even getting up this hill is enjoyable, with a restored antique tram making half the journey and a creaking funicular the other. The city's amusement park at the top is tiny, but the views are spectacular. Behind Tibidabo stretches the wonderful Parc Natural de Collserola *(see p147)*.

>> *Take the cable-car to the top of Monjuïc, then enjoy the stroll back down the verdant slopes*

INTRODUCING BARCELONA

Some of Barcelona's best-known festivals take place in spring and summer. You can enjoy outdoor drama, music and dance in a Greek-style open-air theatre during the prestigious Grec performing arts festival; leap over bonfires on the beach on Midsummer's Night; and party hard with tens of thousands of music fans at the Sónar. Alternatively, join in the fun at old-fashioned neighbourhood festivals, or simply soak up the romance of Lover's Day in April.

La Diada de Sant Jordi

The feast of St George is Lover's Day in Catalunya, when couples traditionally exchange gifts of roses and books. The air is heady with spring and romance, and the streets become a sea of rose petals. There are also outdoor readings from Cervantes' *Don Quixote* in tribute to the chivalrous hero of the book. **24 Apr**

Festival de Música Antigua

www.lacaixa.es/fundacio

The Festival of Early Music takes place in venues such as the beautiful Palau de la Música *(see p98)*. Most atmospheric of all are the concerts held in the Saló del Tinell – a sublime Gothic banqueting hall that's now part of the Museu d'Història de la Ciutat *(see p78)*.

Late Apr/early May

Festival de Flamenco de Ciutat Vella

www.tallerdemusics.com

Flamenco is not part of Catalan culture, but the flood of immigrants from southern Spain has ensured that the spirit of this dance remains vibrant in Barcelona. The flamboyant dancing takes over the streets in the last week of May, with live outdoor performances on the Rambla de Raval. **Late May**

Festa de Sant Joan (Midsummer's Eve)

www.bcn.es/santjoan

Midsummer's Eve on the night of 23 June is explosively celebrated with huge bonfires on the beaches, fireworks – every balcony and terrace seems to crackle with a volley of fizzing rockets – and plenty of cava-fuelled carousing across the city. **Jun**

Sónar

www.sonar.es

During one long, crazy weekend in mid-June (dates vary), Barcelona hosts one of the biggest and slickest festivals of music and multimedia in Spain. Sónar by Day has exhibitions, conferences and record fairs. Sónar by Night, held at venues in Hospital de Llobregat, features

spring and summer

some of the biggest names in electronic music, such as Ryuichi Sakamoto and Massive Attack. **Jun**

Dia per l'Alliberament Lesbià i Gai

On the last Sunday in June, Orgull Gay (Gay Pride) is celebrated with a parade of floats in the city centre and political speeches in front of the City Hall. There are market stalls and live concerts on Plaça Universitat and, of course, plenty of action in the bars and clubs. **End Jun**

Classics als Parcs

www.bcn.es/parcsijardins/act_home.htm

Throughout July, free classical concerts take place in several city parks. Schedules change annually, but Saturday-night concerts (from 10pm) are mostly held in-the Parc de la Ciutadella *(see p143)*. The other main parks involved include La Tamarita (entrance on Passeig de Sant Gervasi), Turó Park (entrances on Avinguda de Pau Casals and C/Josep Bertrand) and Jardins Ca n'Altamira (entrances on C/Horaci and C/Mandri). **Jul**

Festival del Grec

www.bcn.es/grec

Barcelona's biggest festival of performing arts gets its name from Montjuïc's open-air Teatre Grec *(see p100)*, where many of the main performances are staged against a romantic backdrop of ivy-clad stone. Through-out July the festival offers an excellent and wide-ranging programme of theatre and dance, as well as classical, world and contemporary music. All of Barcelona's main venues play host to the performances. **End Jun–early Aug**

Festa Major de Gràcia

www.festamajordegracia.org

Long known for its feisty independence, Gràcia puts on a fantastic show every August during its colourful neighbourhood festival. Each street vies to create the best decorations, and there are parades featuring traditional Catalan *gegants* and *capgrossos* (giants and fatheads). The festival culminates with a wild *correfoc*, when locals dressed up as fire-spitting dragons and demons race through the streets. **Aug**

INTRODUCING BARCELONA

Barcelona kicks off autumn with its best traditional festival, the fabulous, week-long Festes de la Mercè. The seaside barri of Barceloneta puts on a fantastic show for its neighbourhood festival, and jazz-lovers are well catered for at the International Jazz Festival in November. In the run-up to Christmas, the whole city glitters with lights, and outdoor markets spring up selling all kinds of quirky gifts and decorations. And then, at winter's end, there's Carnaval...

Festes de la Mercè
www.bcn.es/merce

The best festival in the city, this is held over a fun-packed week at the end of September. *Gegants* and *capgrossos* (giants and fatheads) lumber through the streets, fire-breathing dragons charge through packed crowds for the city's biggest *correfoc* (fire-run) and, down on the beach, there are dazzling nightly firework spectacles. At the Maremagnum complex overlooking the port, Catalan wine- and cava-producers set out their stalls – for a small admission fee, you can sample and buy a spectacular array of local wine and food. As part of the Festes de la Mercè, the Festa de les Arts a Carrer (Festival of Street Theatre) keeps the streets humming with activity, and the BAM (Barcelona Acció Musical) festival puts on (usually) free outdoor concerts of alternative music. **Sep**

Festa Major de la Barceloneta

The delightfully old-fashioned barri of Barceloneta celebrates its own neighbourhood festival around the end of September (dates vary) by transforming its narrow streets into magical stages, hung with bizarre canopies made of all kinds of unusual junk. The festa is kicked off with a bang by the lumbering figure of Bum Bum, who takes to the streets firing a miniature cannon and scattering sweets. There are live bands and dancing, a huge paella competition and parades of Catalan folkloric figures (giants, dragons and fatheads). **Sep**

International Jazz Festival
www.the-project.net/jazz.htm

Big names from the jazz world converge in Barcelona for this festival during November. The city's finest venues – including L'Auditori *(see p103)* and the Palau de la Música Catalana *(see p98)* – host the main events, but there are concerts across the city and free performances in the Parc de la Ciutadella *(see p143)*. **Nov**

Fira de Santa Llúcia

The feast day of Santa Llúcia on the 1 December marks the official beginning of the Christmas season, and the start of the Christmas market. The expansive

autumn and winter

Plaça Nova in front of the Cathedral is crammed with stalls selling handmade gifts and decorations. Most are filled with typical figures made for nativity scenes, including the curious Catalan figure of the *cagoner*, who wears a scarlet beret and squats, bottom bared, with a blissful expression. **Dec**

Cavalcada de Reis

This is one for the kids: traditionally, the Three Kings bring gifts for good children on 6 January. Every year on the evening of 5 January, the Three Kings arrive by boat in the Port Vell and set off on a parade up Las Ramblas and around the city, scattering sweets as they go. It's a theatrical affair, with live camels and elaborate floats. **Jan**

Calçotada
Train to Valls (75 mins) from Barcelona Sants

Barcelonins are enthusiastic foodies: *bolets* (wild mushrooms) throw them into ecstasies, while the humble *calçot* (a cross between a leek and an onion) generates quasi-religious fervour. Between January and March,

city folk descend on the rural market town of Valls, home of the *calçot*, to enjoy the Calçotada. This traditional feast honours the tasty vegetable, which is roasted until black (peel off the outer leaves before eating), and served up in newspaper with a *romesco* (tomato and garlic) sauce. The Calçotada has become a fixture at restaurants in Valls, and the town's festivities are at their height on the last Sunday of January. **Jan–Mar**

Carnaval
www.bcn.es/carnaval

Carnaval (usually February, but dates vary) is opened by Sa Magestat Carnestoltes (the Carnival King), followed by the exuberant Gran Rúa (Grand Parade) with prizes for the winning float. Typical Catalan sausage *butifarra* is handed out, and markets host *larderos* ("feasts of fatty foods"). The fun ends on Ash Wednesday, the first day of Lent, when the effigy of the Carnival King is ceremonially burnt, and the curious and ancient ceremony of the Enterrament de la Sardina (Burial of the Sardine) takes place on the beach. **Feb/Mar**

Public transport in Barcelona is cheap, reliable and easy to use. The metro is clean, safe and efficient, allowing access to most parts of the city and key sights. Bus routes are extensive and regular, and trains are smart and punctual. Road traffic, on the other hand, is nightmarish and, unless you plan to make frequent trips out of town, there is little point in hiring a car. Barcelona's centre – the Ciutat Vella (Old City) – is compact, and best negotiated on foot.

Arrival

Barcelona is served by two international airports. **El Prat** is the bigger of the two and closer to the city centre (about 20 minutes by taxi); it has three terminals. The **Girona-Costa Brava** airport is located nearly 100 km (60 miles) from Barcelona, but is popular because budget airline **Ryanair** flies there.

El Prat (Barcelona Airport)

The **Aerobús** service runs between the airport (with stops at all three terminals) and Plaça de Catalunya (Map 4 F1) in the city centre. Buses run every 12 minutes from around 6am to midnight. The journey time is 35–45 minutes, and a single fare will cost you less than €4.

Trains to and from the airport stop at Sants, Plaça de Catalunya, Arc de Triomf and Clot-Aragó – all of which are on the metro network. Trains run every 30 minutes in each direction, from around 6am to 11pm, and journey times take 18–23 minutes. A single fare is less than €3.

A taxi from the airport to the city centre costs €15–25 on weekdays, €17–30 at weekends, at night and on public holidays, including airport tax. There is also a small supplement charged per item of luggage.

Girona-Costa Brava Airport

Ryanair runs a **bus service** from Girona airport to Barcelona city centre, which is open to everybody, no matter which carrier you've used. Bus times are co-ordinated with flight departure and arrival times. In Barcelona, buses arrive and depart from Estació del Nord, and its nearest metro stop is Arc de Triomf. The journey time is about 70 minutes. A 30-day return costs around €20; a single a little over half that amount.

Getting Around

The metro is generally the quickest and most straightforward way of getting around central Barcelona. Buses and urban trains are useful for areas not served by the metro, and overland trains are excellent for day excursions to Sitges, Montserrat, Girona and further afield.

TMB (Transports Metropolitans de Barcelona)

TMB manages all inner city transport, including the metro, buses, trams and the Funicular de Montjuïc. Its website has an English-language version, and provides maps and a useful journey planner. Information points are dotted throughout the city at the following metro stops: Universitat and Diagonal (both 8am–8pm Mon–Fri); Sants-Estació and Sagrada Família (both 7am–9pm Mon–Fri).

Barcelona's various modes of public transport have an integrated ticketing policy within the central urban area. A single ticket for the metro, buses, trams and trains within the centre costs under €1.50. However, multiple-trip travel cards are better value. They give access to the metro, buses, trams and trains (RENFE and FGC), and allow for transfers from one to another. The **T-10** ("Te-diez") costs little more than €6, and allows 10 trips on any means of public transport. Groups travelling together can share it by stamping it once per person at designated machines when entering the metro station, on a train platform, or when boarding a bus or tram. As with other integrated tickets, the T-10 allows transfer from one mode of transport to others within a 75-minute period (just re-validate your ticket as you change). Single tickets do not allow for transfers.

T-10 tickets can be bought from machines or the ticket office in metro and train stations, as well as at selected newsagents. On buses you can buy only single tickets. Note that the fares quoted above are for tickets for travel within zone 1, which covers central Barcelona and parts of the outskirts. If you're travelling outside zone 1, fares increase accordingly.

Metro

The metro lines are numbered 1 to 5 and each is identified by a different colour. Metros start running at about

5am and stop around midnight during the week, 2am Fridays and Saturdays.

Buses

Buses start running at 5:30am and continue until around 11pm. Most of the 16 city Nitbus (night bus) routes pass through Plaça de Catalunya. They run from 10:30pm to 4:30–6am every night. For detailed bus routes, go to one of the **TMB** information points or visit their website.

RENFE Trains

Barcelona's main railway station (where most long-distance and local services stop) is **Sants-Estació,** though many of the trains also stop at Passeig de Gràcia, Plaça de Catalunya, Arc de Triomf and Clot-Aragó.

FGC Trains

The Catalan regional railway is known as FGC (Ferrocarrils de la Generalitat de Catalunya). It connects the city centre with Barcelona's outer limits, such as Tibidabo. This is also the network you need if heading for Montserrat *(see p148)* – take an FGC train from Plaça Espanya.

Trams

Barcelona's newest form of transport comprises four tram lines that stretch westwards from Plaça Francesc Macià towards Zona Universitaria, and south from Ciutadella-Vila Olímpica metro station to Sant Adrià, via Glòries to El Maresme. You can use the same tickets as on metros and buses, and trams have the advantage of being completely wheelchair-accessible.

Taxis

Barcelona's yellow-and-black taxis are plentiful and cheap – the minimum fare is around €1.50. They can be hailed on the street, providing their green light is on, and there are many taxi ranks at the main transport terminals and at squares across the city. Credit cards are seldom accepted, and most drivers do not carry more than €20 in change.

Other Forms Of Transport

In summer, **"Trixi" rickshaws** are a popular way for tourists to see the sights at a leisurely pace. They can be hailed, but most gather at the main tourist sights in the Old City. Rickshaws charge around €1.70 per km, or can be booked for hour or half-hour tours of the city (€20 and €11, respectively).

There are an increasing number of bicycle-hire companies. **Un Cotxe Menys** in the Barri Gòtic rent out bicycles from €5/hour or €15/day.

Tours

Gourmet tapas and walking tours, wine tastings, picnics and boat trips, and visits to the outlying wine regions are available though **Saboroso**. There are also innumerable companies offering sightseeing tours of the city. Try **Barcelona Walking Tours** for all things Gaudì or Picasso related.

Un Cotxe Menys do "made-to-measure" guided bike tours of Barcelona, while scheduled bike tours leave from Plaça Sant Jaume at 11am daily. The cost is €22 per person, and you simply have to turn up 10 minutes before the start to join the tour.

Directory

Aerobús Service
93 415 6020 / 010

Airports
El Prat Airport Information
93 298 3838

Girona Airport Information
97 218 6600

For comprehensive information (in English) about all Spanish airports, browse:
www.aena.es

Barcelona Walking Tours
93 285 3834
(tours leave daily from the Tourist Office at Plaça Catalunya)

Un Cotxe Menys
C/Espartería 3
93 268 2105

FGC
93 205 1515
www.fgc.net

RENFE
National trains: 90 224 0202
International trains: 90 224 3402
www.renfe.es

Ryanair
www.ryanair.com

Ryanair Bus Service
90 236 1550

Saboroso
66 777 0492 • www.saboroso.com

Taxis
Institut Metropolità del Taxi
93 223 5151 • www.emt-amb.com
Ràdio Taxi
93 303 3033
Servi Taxi
93 330 0300

TMB (Transports Metropolitans de Barcelona)
93 318 7074 • www.tmb.net

Trams (Trambaix)
90 219 3275 • www.trambcn.com

Trixi Rickshaws
93 310 1379 • www.trixi.com

Barcelona is an easy city to get around, and its infrastructure for visitors is constantly being improved. The tourist office supplies plenty of information on the city's sights and entertainments, has a good network of professional guides and offers a bargain selection of discounted passes for sightseeing and travel.

Disabled Travellers

The **Institut Municipal de Persones amb Disminució** can provide information on wheelchair-friendly bars, restaurants, museums and theatres. **ECOM** is a federation of organizations for the disabled that can provide information on accommodation and venues with specially adapted facilities. The **Centre d'Informació de Transport Adaptat** has a Spanish-speaking disabled transport information phone line (93 486 0752) for details on wheelchair access on metros and buses.

Emergencies and Health

If you are the victim of a crime, contact the closest *comisaría* (police station) to report it. You need to file a *denuncia* (an official report of the crime) to make an insurance claim. The **Policía Nacional** mainly deal with robberies and attacks. Their emergency number is **091**. You can call this or the general emergency number (**112**) to locate the nearest *comisaría*. For an ambulance, dial **061**. In the case of a medical emergency, anyone can go to the casualty department of the main **public hospitals**. Centre d'Urgències Perecamps (Av Drassanes 13–15) and Hospital Clínic (C/Vilarroel 170) are the most central and are both open 24 hours daily. EU citizens can claim free medical attention with a European health insurance card (which recently

replaced the E111 form). It must be obtained before travelling. Non-EU nationals can make use of the public health services on a paying basis.

Gay and Lesbian Travellers

Barcelona is a well-established destination for gay travellers, particularly in the "Gay Eixample" (Eixample Esquerra), and 45 minutes up the coast is the gay mecca of Sitges *(see pp138–9)*. The lesbian scene is less upfront but no less welcoming. **Telèfon Rosa** (900 601 601; 7–10pm daily) is a free phone line for help and advice on gay and lesbian issues. Most magazines and resources are in Spanish but, if you frequent the Eixample Esquerra, you'll find flyers and freebies promoting events and club nights in most bars.

Listings/What's On

Weekly *La Guía del Ocio* can be picked up at any newsagent for €1. The guide has detailed listings for theatre, cinema, restaurants, arts and entertainment. It is available online at **www.guiadelociobcn.es.** Hip weekly guide *Time Out Barcelona* is also available online at **www.timeout.com/barcelona**. It has a good round-up of the week's highlights. Barcelona's premier English-language monthly magazine, *Barcelona Metropolitan* (**www.barcelona-metropolitan.com**),

delivers a slice of expatriate life in the Catalan capital. Check out the bilingual **www.lecool.com** for the scoop on the best of the city's nightlife.

Money

Although most banks accept euro travellers' cheques (for a commission and with a passport as ID), you'll get a better exchange rate if you use your debit or credit card at one of the many ATMs that are scattered liberally about the city. Most hotels, restaurants and shops accept credit cards, and in many you use your PIN along with a bank card.

Opening Hours

Most **shops** open at 9:30 or 10am and close between 8 and 9pm. Many stay open all day, though smaller and less central shops close for lunch (1:30 or 2pm until 4 or 5pm) and on Saturday afternoons. Most shops do not open on Sundays or public holidays.

Banks are generally open 8:30–2 Mon–Fri; between October and April, many banks also open 8:30–1 Sat. The majority of **post offices** open 8:30–2:30 Mon–Fri and 9:30–1 Sat; many open weekday afternoons as well, often without closing for lunch.

When it comes to entertainment, Barcelona gets going late and stays out later. Few locals eat much before 9:30 at night, and second sittings can be as late as 11pm. **Restaurants** tend to be open from 1:30 or 2 to 4 or 4:30 for lunch, and around 9 to 11pm or midnight for dinner (later on weekends).

Bars vary greatly in their opening times. In the evening, some open as early as 7, some as late as 11 or even midnight (the majority are somewhere in the middle). Closing times tend to be more uniform: 2 or 2:30am between Sunday and Thursday, and 3am on Friday and Saturday. **Clubs** don't generally start filling up until 2 or 3am, when the bars have closed. Club closing times range from 5 to 7am.

Many shops, restaurants, cafés and bars close for all or part of August.

Phones and Communications

Public phones in Barcelona commonly take coins, telephone cards and credit cards; many have multilingual displays. Centres for cheap long-distance calls are dotted around town (especially in the Raval), and most newsagents and *tabacs* (tobacconists) sell an array of discounted phone cards. Using your own mobile phone in Spain is easy with most European and some US networks – check with your service provider before travelling. If you need to hire a phone, try **Rent a Phone**. Barcelona has a plethora of Internet cafés, such as **easyEverything** and **Locutorios**. And if you use a laptop or Internet phone, **www.wififreespot.com/europe.html** lists places where there is free wireless Internet connectivity.

Security

Bag snatching is a common problem in Barcelona, especially in the small streets of the Barri Gòtic and the Born. Try not to carry valuables or large amounts of cash, and keep photo-copies of your passport and credit cards in a safe place at your hotel.

Tipping

Catalans tend to tip very little. Service is officially included on the bill in **restaurants** – if you want to tip, however, 5 to 10% is plenty. In **bars**, customers might leave some small change at most. Tipping in **taxis** is not very common but, again, many people leave some small change or round up the fare. It is standard to tip **hotel porters,** though – a euro or two is usually sufficient.

Tourist Information

The main tourist office is underneath Plaça de Catalunya (Map 4 F1), and is open 9–9 daily. As well as general tourist information, it has Internet access, money exchange facilities and a hotel booking service. You can also buy tourist tickets for discounted access to the city's top sights.

The **Barcelona Card** offers 2–5 days' unlimited access to buses, metros, trams and urban trains, reduced fares on the airport bus and the Funicular de Montjuïc, and discounts to many museums, shops, shows and restaurants. Its cost ranges from €23 (for 2 days) to €34 (5 days).

The **Articket** gives half-price entry to seven of Barcelona's top museums. It costs €15 and is valid for 3 months. You can also purchase it online at **www.telentrada.com**.

The **Barcelona Bus Turístic** ticket gives unlimited access to the double-decker tourist buses for one or two days (€18 and €22 respectively). Simply jump on or off at any of the 42 stops. The ticket is also valid on three other designated tourist routes.

Directory

24-hour Pharmacy
Farmàcia Clapés
Las Ramblas
98 93 301 2843

Directory Enquiries
International Directory Enquiries:
11825
National Directory Enquiries:
11818

easyEverything
Las Ramblas 31, Barri Gòtic
93 318 2435
www.easyeverything.com

ECOM
Gran Via de les Corts
Catalanes 562 principal 2ª
93 451 5550
www.ecom.es

Gay & Lesbian websites
www.naciongay.com
www.guiagay.com
www.mensual.com

Institut Municipal de Persones amb Disminució
Avenida Diagonal 233,
93 413 2775
www.bcn.es/imd

Locutorios (phone and Internet centre)
C/Hospital 17, El Raval
93 318 9739

Lost or Stolen Credit Cards
(24-hour phone lines with English-speaking operators)
American Express *902 375 6370*
Diners Club *901 10 10 11*
MasterCard *900 97 12 31*
VISA *900 99 11 24*

Main Tourist Office
Plaça de Catalunya (On the El Corte Inglés side of the square)
Opening hours: 9–9 daily
93 285 3834
www.barcelonaturisme.com

Rent a Phone
C/Numància 212
www.rphone.es

restaurants

Spanish regional cooking is well represented in and around the city, with hundreds of traditional restaurants serving delicious local dishes, as well as the cuisines of Galicia, Asturias and the Basque Country. The Eixample is best for high-class dining; Barri Gòtic, the Raval and Born for trendy eateries. Barceloneta has excellent fish restaurants, while Gràcia is good for a range of ethnic cuisines.

RESTAURANTS

Barcelona's dining scene has undergone a sea change of late. The age-old reliance on prime-quality ingredients has been preserved thankfully, but whereas that fillet of tender monkfish was once presented fried and unadorned, it might now come drizzled in citrus oil, or poached in coconut milk and accompanied with a lime and coriander foam. It's this matching of tradition and a modern appetite that makes the city's restaurants unique and so appealing.

Sally Davies

Seafood

The former maritime district of Barceloneta is a natural home to most of the city's seafood restaurants, and **Can Solé** *(see p35)* is one of the best. The paellas are legendary at nearby **Set Portes** *(see p35)*, while **La Paradeta** *(see p32)* is both a fishmonger's and a simple canteen for eating fresh fish, cooked as you like, at rock-bottom prices.

New-Wave Catalan

Inspired (and often trained) by celebrated chef Ferran Adrià at **El Bulli** *(see p47)*, molecular gastronomists are a feature of Barcelona's kitchens these days. For new and often startling takes on traditional local cuisine try **Comerç 24** *(see p32)*, **Moo** *(see p42)* and **Ot** *(see p43)*. Less reliant on Adrià's techniques but equally surprising is **Cinc Sentits** *(see p39)*.

Alfresco Dining

On a sunny afternoon, it's hard to beat the beachside terraces of **Bestial** *(see p37)* and nearby **Agua** *(see p36)*, but for a romantic outdoor dinner date try the **Cafè de l'Acadèmia** *(see p29)*, with its tables set out on a delightful little square, or the leafy gardens of **Can Travi Nou** *(see p45)*, situated high above the city.

choice eats

Tapas

The concept of tapas has only recently been imported to Catalunya from elsewhere in Spain, and here tends to take the form of *platillos* (small plates, designed to be shared). Try them at **Mosquito** *(see p31)*, **Comerç 24** *(see p32)*, **Ginger** *(see p111)* and **Mam i Teca** *(see p117)*. For more traditional fare, head to **Taller de Tapas** *(see p30)*.

Traditional Catalan

Classics of Catalan cuisine are served with a luxurious modern touch (and in a Gaudí-designed building, no less) at **Casa Calvet** *(see p38)*. **Can Culleretes** *(see p28)* serves simpler versions in rooms dating back over 200 years. **Pitarra** *(see p29)* specializes in rich game, while **Los Caracoles** *(see p29)* is best known for its eponymous snails.

Top-Drawer Restaurants

Catalunya has become something of a firmament of Michelin stars in recent years – **El Bulli** *(see p47)*, **Sant Pau** *(see p46)* and **Racó de Can Fabes** *(see p45)* lead the pack with three apiece. Equally accomplished is the wonderful **Celler de Can Roca** *(see p46)* in Girona, with Barcelona's **Alkimia** *(see p37)* and **Abac** *(see p31)* not far behind.

Can Culleretes *the city's oldest restaurant*

C/Quintana 5 • 93 317 3022
»» www.culleretes.com Open lunch & dinner
Tue–Sat, lunch only Sun; closed July

This well-loved Barri Gòtic restaurant has been feeding the folk of Barcelona since 1786. The cavernous dining rooms ooze character, while the menu concentrates on Catalan classics, such as goose and pears, and suckling pig with pine nuts and raisins. **Cheap**

Arc Café *all day snacks for bohemians*

C/Carabassa 19 • 93 302 5204
Open lunch & dinner daily

Tucked away down a tiny side street, the Arc Café possesses an air of bonhomie that has made it a popular haunt of Barcelona's intellectuals. Artists, film-makers, writers and musicians all gather here for high-brow discussions and world cuisine. The café's curry specials are a particular favourite. **Cheap**

Schilling *wine and snacks, day and night*

C/Ferran 23 • 93 317 6787
Open 10am–2:30am Mon–Sat, noon–2am Sun

Barcelona has never had grand cafés of the type boasted by Madrid, but Schilling does its damnedest to fill the gap, its *belle époque* look setting off the contemporary art that lines the walls. A mixed crowd – gay, straight, tourist, local – is drawn in by tapas, toasted snacks and good-looking waiting staff. **Cheap**

Govinda *vegetarian Indian*

Plaça Vila de Madrid 4 • 93 318 7729
Open lunch & dinner Tue–Sat, lunch only Mon & Sun

A zippier alternative to the generally uninspired vegetarian restaurants in Barcelona, Govinda offers tasty curries, home-made bread, lassis and *chai* (spiced milk tea) to mainly students and backpackers passing through the barrio. The lunchtime fixed menu is excellent value, and there's a decent salad bar. **Cheap**

Les Quinze Nits *Mediterranean bargains*

Plaça Reial 6 • 93 317 3075
Open lunch & dinner daily

Queues snaking across Plaça Reial are testament to the winning combination of cheap dishes and the consummately elegant surroundings of Quinze Nits. Plump for the fresh salads and unfussy meat dishes here and you won't go wrong; fish and paella, however, are not the restaurant's forte. **Cheap**

Café de l'Acadèmia *modern Catalan* `6 E4`
C/Lledó 1 • 93 319 8253
Open breakfast, lunch & dinner Mon–Fri

Hugely popular with workers from nearby City Hall, this cosy, bare-bricked restaurant offers a modern take on rich and gamey Catalan favourites. Its risotto with *foie* (*see p31*) is a stalwart of the menu, along with duck, served in myriad ways. Arrive early to grab an outside table in the shadow of Sant Just church. **Moderate**

Los Caracoles *traditional spit-roast chicken* `5 C4`
C/Escudellers 14 • 93 302 3185
Open lunch & dinner daily

This famous restaurant is renowned for its chicken, which is spit-roasted on the corner of the street. The rest of the food is adequate, but the main reason to visit is for a look around some of Barcelona's most fabulous dining rooms – a warren of wood-panelled, colourfully tiled, bow-beamed grottoes. **Moderate**

El Salón *creative Mediterranean* `6 E4`
C/Hostal d'en Sol 6–8 • 93 315 2159
Open dinner only Mon–Sat

Hidden down a side street behind the post office, El Salón manages to be both wonderfully cosy and permanently animated, with a mixed, fun crowd. The look is boho Baroque, and the menu similarly eclectic – guinea fowl with cloves and chestnuts, lamb cous-cous and maybe apple crumble for dessert. **Moderate**

Pitarra *classic Catalan* `5 D4`
C/Avinyó 56 • 93 301 1647
>> www.pitarra.com Open lunch & dinner Tue–Sat

This friendly Catalan restaurant was once the head-quarters of revolutionary poet Frederic Soler "Pitarra" and his cronies. The cooking is unapologetically old fashioned, offering traditional dishes, such as *escalivada* (roasted peppers and aubergines), rich fish stews, and creamy, stuffed cannelloni. **Moderate**

Restaurants

Taller de Tapas *classic Spanish tapas*

5 D3

Plaça Sant Josep Oriol 9 • 93 301 8020

>> www.tallerdetapas.com Open noon–midnight daily

Barcelona waited a long time to get a bar worthy of a whole evening's snacking. Taller (meaning workshop) fits the bill nicely, offering a superb range of classically Spanish snacks, from chorizo and tortilla to steaming bowls of chickpeas and spinach, seafood and steak *montaditos* (open sandwiches). **Cheap**

Dionisos *lively Greek*

6 G4

Avinguda Marquès de l'Argentera 27 • 93 268 7690

>> www.dionisos.ws Open lunch & dinner daily

With a prettily decorated dining room that's full of character, and a terrace offering pleasant views across to the park, Dionisos is lively, but not in a plate-smashing kind of way. All the Greek culinary classics are well prepared and presented, including succulent stuffed vine leaves and creamy moussaka. **Cheap**

Els Quatre Gats *historic restaurant*

6 E2

C/Montsió 3 • 93 302 4140

>> www.4gats.com Open 1pm–1am daily

"The Four Cats" was opened in 1897 by Pere Romeu, a minor artist who wanted to emulate the bistros and drinking dens of Paris. A disastrous businessman, Romeu had to be supported financially by his friends, among them the highly regarded Catalan artists Ramon Casas, Santiago Rusiñol, and the young Picasso (the fourth cat), who staged his first exhibition here and designed the menu cover too.

Prized also for its architecture (the building was designed by the great Modernista architect Puig I Cadafalch), Els Quatre Gats has become one of the city's most emblematic restaurants. Despite its place on the well-trodden tourist trail, the food is good, particularly the slow-roasted suckling lamb and salt-baked fish. The atmosphere is unreservedly kitsch, with billowing flower arrangements, an army of liveried waiters and a house pianist. **Moderate**

Mosquito *exotic tapas*   `6 G3`

C/Carders 46 • 93 268 7569
>> www.mosquitotapas.com
Open lunch & dinner Tue–Sun

Mosquito brings together classic recipes from all over Asia and presents them in the tapas format – dishes small enough to allow a wide selection. Expect fried pork with rice-noodle cakes, Hong Kong ribs and gyoza dumplings filled with aubergine and basil. **Cheap**

Abac *top-class French-Mediterranean*   `6 G4`

C/Rec 79-89 • 93 319 6600
>> www.restaurantabac.com
Open lunch & dinner only Tue–Sat, dinner only Mon

Known in Barcelona as the chef's chef, Xavier Pellicer pairs Gallic and Basque influences in this slightly austere Michelin-starred restaurant. An emphasis on the game is evident in the rich and creamy dishes, and there's an outstanding cheeseboard too. **Expensive**

Espai Sucre *the first pudding restaurant*   `6 F3`

C/Princesa 53 • 93 268 1630
>> www.espaisucre.com Open dinner only Tue–Sat

Misleadingly named, the "Sugar Space" is not merely for the sweet of tooth. Apart from a short list of "entrées", the menu is indeed devoted to puddings – but they are a far cry from traditional desserts. Think more along the lines of eucalyptus ice cream served in lychee soup. **Expensive**

Catalan Cuisine

The cuisine of Catalunya is recognized as among the best regional food in Spain. There are 36 Michelin-starred restaurants in the region, several of them in Barcelona, but it is the country bistros, beach bars and food festivals that retain the heart of Catalan cuisine.

Robust peasant fare has always played a big role in the cuisine of the region, from richly satisfying *botifarra* (coarse Catalan sausage) served with *mongetes* (white beans) to *mar y montaña* – an inspired take on "surf and turf", combining elements of the land with those of the sea, such as rabbit with lobster, prepared in a rich saffron sauce. Another example of rustic fare is the ubiquitous *pa amb tomàquet* (dense country bread, toasted and rubbed with a vine-ripened tomato and pungent garlic, then drizzled with fine olive oil). Catalunya is also known for its sunset-coloured *suquets* (rich fish and seafood stews) and for sumptuous rice dishes. One of the best is *arros negre* – Valencia rice with chunks of creamy cuttlefish and clams in a rich sauce of black cuttlefish ink, served with a dollop of the region's famous *alioli* (an oily, garlicky dip). You are also likely to see *foie* on a Catalan menu. As distinct from foie gras, *foie* is a liver of duck, goose or rabbit, semi-cooked and seasoned with salt or liqueur.

Then there are the desserts, such as *crema catalana* (luscious vanilla custard with a burnt sugar crust), pears poached in spiced red wine and *mel i mató* (soft curd cheese drizzled with honey).

Calçotada, at the end of January, is one of the region's most riotous food festivals. Vast quantities of *calçots* (a cross between a spring onion and a leek) are consumed, having been chargrilled on vine cuttings. They are dunked in a dense pepper and almond sauce and washed down with lots of cava.

Restaurants

Comerç 24 *designer tapas*

6 G2

C/Comerç 24 • 93 319 2102
»» www.comerc24.com Open lunch & dinner Tue–Sat

When foodies get excited about Catalunya's gastro-nomic revolution, Comerç 24 is one of their first points of reference. Designers, too, wax lyrical about its achingly hip steely grey interior.

Chef Carles Abellan spent nine years working with the legendary Ferran Adrià at El Bulli *(see p47)*. The influence is easily discerned in dishes such as tempura served with a soy sauce "foam". As at El Bulli, food is served in small *platillos* (a sophisticated form of tapas). The result is playful, surprising and yet faithful to its Catalan roots, as exemplified by a dessert based on the traditional tea-time snack of bread and chocolate – here lightly fried in olive oil with sea salt. Sea urchins, a local delicacy, are served with "*quinoa*" – actually, granulated foie-gras ice cream. Test the skills of the kitchen by ordering the Menú Festival – a selection of its most adventurous dishes. **Expensive**

La Paradeta *seafood canteen*

6 G4

C/Comercial 7 • 93 268 1939
»» www.laparadeta.com
Open lunch Sat & Sun, dinner Tue–Sat

Somewhere between a fishmonger's and a restaurant, La Paradeta displays sparklingly fresh seafood on a bank of crushed ice. Point at what you want, take a ticket and collect it once the fish has been prepared – simply steamed or grilled. **Moderate**

Cal Pep *venerable seafood tapas bar*

6 F4

Plaça de les Olles 8 • 93 310 7961
»» www.calpep.com
Open lunch Tue–Sat, dinner Mon–Sat; closed Aug & Easter

Make sure you arrive early in order to bag a seat at the counter. There is a dining room at the back, but it would be a pity to miss the show, as the esteemed Pep Manubens and his team chop, toss, fry and slice some of the tastiest seafood in Barcelona. **Moderate**

Good value   For the very latest on Barcelona go to »» www.realcity.dk.com

Gente de Pasta *trendy Italian* `6 G3`
Passeig de Picasso 10 • 93 268 7017
>> www.gentedepasta.com Open lunch & dinner daily

A multi-tasking restaurant-bar-club, aimed squarely at the young and hip, Gente de Pasta boasts silver walls, see-and-be-seen windows and DJ waiters. A long and frequently changing list of spaghettis, rigatonis, pennes and risottos is complemented by a good-value set menu at lunch time. **Cheap**

Habana Vieja *Cuban soul food* `6 F4`
C/Banys Vells 2 • 93 268 2504
Open lunch & dinner Mon–Sat

"Old Havana" is one of the cosiest restaurants in town, both buzzing and intimate, with an uplifting sound-track that provides everything you'd expect from a Cuban restaurant. Try *ropa vieja* (shredded beef) or *arroz congrí* (rice with beans), accompanied by fried plantain and, naturally, Mojito cocktails. **Moderate**

Little Italy *Mediterranean, with jazz* `6 G3`
C/Rec 30 • 93 319 7973
>> www.restaurantlittleitaly.com Open lunch & dinner daily

Offering a taste of downtown in boho Born, this split-level dining room captures the New York spirit with surprising aplomb. Smoky decor, jazz tunes (live music Mon, Tue & Wed) and a generally cheery atmosphere give Little Italy an upbeat vibe, while the gutsy pasta dishes are food for the soul. **Moderate**

L'Ou Com Balla *French-Moroccan* `6 F4`
C/Banys Vells 20 • 93 310 5378
Open dinner daily

Intimate is the word for this pint-sized restaurant, with tightly placed tables, low lighting, dark wood furniture and the romantic flicker of candlelight. An eccentric menu uses themed ingredients – chocolate, say, or aubergine – that turn up in every dish from starters to pudding. Pleasant and quirky. **Moderate**

El Convent *hearty market fare*

`5 C2`

C/Jerusalem 3 • 93 317 1052

>> www.elconvent.com Open lunch & dinner Mon–Sat

Tucked behind the Boqueria *(see p131)* on the site of a former convent, this is an especially popular spot for lunch, so you'll need to arrive early (by 1pm) or queue. A few chandeliers and gilt-framed paintings remain, otherwise El Convent is as unpretentious as the grilled meats and stews it serves. **Cheap**

Ra *hip terrace café*

`5 B2`

Plaça de la Gardunya 3 • 93 301 4163

>> www.ratown.com

Open all day Mon–Sat, lunch only Sun

The popularity of Ra is such that each lunch time sees a queue snaking down the street in eager anticipation. But Ra's greatest strength is its breakfasts, where waffles and fry-ups are served, with smoothies, milk-shakes and a panoply of teas and coffees. **Cheap**

Sésamo *cosy vegetarian*

`3 D2`

C/Sant Antoni Abat 52 • 93 441 6411

>> www.sesamo-bcn.com

Open lunch & dinner Wed–Mon

One of the first places in the city to treat vegetarian and vegan food seriously, this tiny restaurant serves up an imaginative menu. The eclectic range of dishes in-cludes nut rissoles and quiches, aubergine caviar and home-made gnocchi, as well as organic wines. **Cheap**

És *modern Mediterranean*

`5 B1`

C/Doctor Dou 14 • 93 301 0068

Open lunch & dinner daily

The crisp, snowy-white dining room and cocktail bar are very now (in Barcelona, at least), but the restau-rant's cuisine is a reassuring mix of the traditional and the vogueish. A youthful crowd samples sea bass carpaccio with wild mushrooms, and follows it up with good old-fashioned *crema catalana*. **Moderate**

Biblioteca *modern European*   `5 B3`
C/Junta de Comerç 28 • 93 412 6221
Open lunch & dinner Tue–Sat; closed 2 weeks in Feb
& 2 weeks in Aug

Basque chef Iñaki López and his Irish partner serve refreshingly unpretentious food that melds tastes and traditions from Britain, Spain and the rest of the Mediterranean. The open kitchen and shelves stacked with cookery books convey a love of food. **Moderate**

Casa Leopoldo *traditional seafood*   `5 B3`
C/Sant Rafael 24 • 93 441 6942
Open lunch & dinner Tue–Sat, lunch only Sun

A long-time favourite with writers, politicians and artists, Casa Leopoldo has legendary status among seafood restaurants, and even features in several novels. It remains beautifully old-school, from its beams and bullfighting posters down to the unadorned simplicity with which the fish is served. **Expensive**

Can Solé *supreme paella*   `4 G5`
C/Sant Carles 4 • 93 221 5012
>> www.restaurantcansole.com Open lunch & dinner
Tue–Sat, lunch only Sun; closed 2 weeks in Aug

Founded in 1903, this is one of Barcelona's classic seafood restaurants. It is also one of the few places that serve paella perfectly – at room temperature, with rice that is sensuous, crispy at the bottom and deeply infused with saffron and seafood. **Expensive**

Set Portes *historic setting*   `6 F5`
Passeig d'Isabel II 14, Barceloneta • 93 319 3033
>> www.7portes.com Open 1pm–1am daily

If walls could talk, those at Set Portes could divulge secrets of the rich and famous, as well as the battle plans of politicians and generals. Since 1836, anyone who's anyone has journeyed from far and wide to sample its famous paellas. Fish soup, salt cod and meat dishes also feature on the menu. **Expensive**

>> *For more on Barcelona's food festivals,* see pp16–19

Arola *playful dishes to share*

Hotel Arts, C/Marina 19–21 • 93 483 8090
>> www.arola-arts.com
Open lunch & dinner Wed–Sun; closed Jan

One of the youngest chefs in Spain to be awarded two Michelin stars, Sergi Arola has become a gastronomic phenomenon with his Madrid restaurant La Broche. Now he flies over to Barcelona once a week to oversee his eponymous restaurant in the Hotel Arts.

The concept of the restaurant is to take traditional tapas and *pica pica* (finger food to share), and to turn them into nouvelle versions of the old favourites. Tapas bar stalwart *patatas bravas*, for example, has become tiny potato moulds piped full of spicy sauce and mayonnaise, while, in Arola's hands, the humble sardine is smoked and served with a seaweed dressing and red wine reduction.

A music policy that serves up retro lounge, funk and nightly DJ sessions contributes to the slick ambience, attracting a well-heeled, young clientele. **Expensive**

Agua *laid-back beach restaurant*

Passeig Marítim 30 • 93 225 1272
>> www.aguadeltragaluz.com Open lunch & dinner daily

Good food on Barcelona's seafront can be frustratingly hard to come by, so Agua has become a welcome addition to the scene, especially for those who wish to see and be seen by the "in" crowd. The glass front-age, seaside terrace and quality Mediterranean dishes make it a favourite, day or night. **Moderate**

Coffee Time

If you are searching for a café with ambience, the Born and the Barri Gòtic neighbourhoods are Barcelona's top contenders. The terraces at **Tèxtil Café** in the Museu Tèxtil *(see p80)* and at **Café d'Estiu** at the Museu Frederic Marès *(see p79)* are hidden within the palatial Gothic courtyards of their respective museums; both are wonderfully atmospheric places for recharging the batteries. **Kasparo** (Plaça Vicenç Martorell 4) in the Raval provides a more upbeat atmosphere and welcome shade beneath its arches. It's also great for parents travelling with kids thanks to a play area situated in the grassy park out front. **Daguiri** (C/Grau i Torras 59) in Barceloneta is a handy precursor to a day on the beach, or a sundowner at the day's end.

Alkimia *stylish fusion* `2 G3`
C/Indústria 79 • 93 207 6115
Open lunch & dinner Mon–Fri

Praise has been lavished upon this smart, sleek, elegantly designed restaurant since it opened at the start of 2003. Unfazed by such attention, chef Jordi Vilà remains focused, delivering A-grade dishes that are clever, but not alienating. At the end of 2004, he was rewarded with his first Michelin star.

His menu changes every three months and takes a revisionist approach to traditional Catalan cooking. An unctuous crayfish-laden rice, for example, is softly infused with sweetly piquant nyora peppers and saffron; a dish that upgrades paella with panache. There are also Asian, Italian and French accents in the cooking. Tuna fillets are pan-seared in soy, but served with pesto; roasted turbot comes with a side dish of red onion marmalade. Attention is also paid to local cheeses, which are perfectly ripened and served at room temperature. **Expensive**

A La Menta *portside paella* `7 B5`
Moll del Gregal 20–21 • 93 225 2913
>> www.restaurante-alamenta.com
Open lunch & dinner daily

It doesn't look like much from the outside, but this *arroceria* (rice restaurant) serves the best rice dishes in the Port Olímpic. The modest terrace has views of the boats in the port and the beaches, making it a top spot for long, lazy lunches. **Moderate**

Bestial *sleek Italian bistro* `7 B4`
C/Ramón Trias Fargas 2–4 • 93 224 0407
>> www.bestialdeltragaluz.com Open lunch and dinner daily

No doubt about it, Bestial has the best beachfront terrace in the city, with sleek wood decking running down to the sand just in front of Frank Gehry's fabulous fish sculpture. The food doesn't cause quite such a stir, but the pasta and pizza dishes are perfectly decent. **Moderate**

Xiringuito Escribà *seaside restaurant* `7 C4`
C/Litoral Mar 42, Platja Bogatell • 93 221 0729
Open lunch & dinner Mon–Sat, lunch only Sun; closed for dinner in winter (until Easter)

The Escribà family is Barcelona's very own dynasty of pastry chefs, so it pays to leave room for dessert when dining here. In keeping with the restaurant's beachfront position, the menu is a textbook of seafood dishes, and this is an excellent place for paella. **Moderate**

>> *Coffee chain BraCafe offers specialist coffees, and is loved by locals for a quick pick-me-up*

Restaurants

Casa Calvet *high-class Catalan* 4 H1

C/Casp 48 • 93 412 4012
>> www.casacalvet.es
Open lunch & dinner Mon–Sat; closed Aug

Located in a Gaudí-designed building, this is a smart, intimate and serious restaurant, frequented by well-heeled Catalans. It may not have received the accolades of Barcelona's more famous dining establishments, but it is, nevertheless, one of the best places to sample contemporary Catalan fare.

The menu changes seasonally, and so is likely to include wild mushrooms and truffles in autumn; game during the short winter season; pert salads, soft fruits and goats' cheeses through the summer; and local lobster and seafood as and when the seasons dictate. A handful of house classics crop up time and again, however, such as truffle and duck confit risotto with yogurt ice cream, baked sea bass with sherry reduction and crisped spinach, and potted rabbit loin with pistachio and apricot sauce. **Expensive**

El Japonés *hip sushi bar* 2 E4

Passatge de la Concepció 2 • 93 487 2592
>> www.eljaponesdeltragaluz.com Open lunch & dinner daily

Sushi bars are second only to the wave of trendy tapas bars in this city where small snacky things hold sway. El Japonés attracts a fashionable crowd, who come for a wide range of Japanese fare, ranging from crispy tempura, gyoza dumplings and noodles to sushi and perky fillets of sashimi. **Moderate**

Le Relais de Venise *steak 'n' chips* 2 E4

C/Pau Claris 142 • 93 467 2162
Open lunch & dinner daily

This buzzing French restaurant is a shrine to one dish: entrecôte. Here, the meat is thinly sliced at your table by a waitress in a French maid's uniform, and served with a herby, secret-recipe sauce and a mountain of shoestring fries. To follow, choose from profiteroles, crêpes and a pungent cheeseboard. **Moderate**

Semproniana *whimsical Catalan joint* 1 D4

C/Rosselló 148 • 93 453 1820
Open lunch & dinner Mon–Sat

Housed in an old printing factory, this classy Catalan eatery is loud and lively – both in terms of decor (fans, brash colours, kitsch paintings, mismatched furniture) and clientele. Catalan foodies gather for contemporary dishes such as rabbit and pears, blood sausage lasagne and chocolate "delirium tremens". **Moderate**

Cinc Sentits *top-notch fusion*   `1 D4`
C/Aribau 58 • 93 323 9490
>> www.cincsentits.com Open lunch & dinner Tue–Sat, lunch only Mon; closed Easter & 2 weeks in Aug

Chef Jordi and his sister, sommelier and maitrêsse d' Amèlia Artal, are of Catalan and Canadian stock, and bring the best traditions of both to this ground-breaking restaurant. In its short life, Cinc Sentits has attracted rave reviews, not just from those impressed by the careful sourcing of hard-to-find ingredients, but also from anyone simply looking to relax in the hands of charming, knowledgeable hosts.

The restaurant's name means five senses, and each of the five is stimulated. Easy-going music and the sharp-edged design (all-white with teak furniture and occasional splashes of red) contribute to this, while the food is a veritable celebration of tastes, aromas and textures, often in unexpected combinations. A pre-starter *amuse-bouche* of foie gras rolled in crushed *cantuccini* biscuits with a dab of violet marmalade offers a hint of the formidable *omakase* (surprise tasting menu). This parade of dishes might include oxtail with squid "noodles" and parsnip parmentier, or a poached egg with chanterelle mushrooms, chopped *botifarra* sausage and caramelized leeks. The palate is cleansed with a take on a Sidecar cocktail (lemon curd, brandy foam and orange dust), or a Granny Smith sorbet with tiny cubes of Sauternes sweet wine jelly, floating in a lemon grass infusion. Of the selection of dreamy desserts, baked maple cheesecake with pumpkin jam is to die for, as is the "intense" pear cake with an almond crust, which is served with ginger ice cream.

Cinc Sentits is not solely about food, however, and a great way to discover more about Spanish wines is to opt for the wine pairing to accompany the *omakase*. The selection is impressive, reasonably priced and related with enthusiasm by Amèlia. **Expensive**

Noti *glamorous Mediterranean*

`2 F5`

C/Roger de Llúria 35–7 • 93 342 6673
» www.noti-universal.com
Open lunch & dinner Mon–Fri, dinner only Sat

This outstanding restaurant is housed in an equally amazing building, the former offices of long-defunct newspaper *El Noticiero Universal*. The building won design awards in its 1960s heyday, and Elena Barta and her celebrated chef partner Christian Crespin have been keen to maintain the aesthetic emphasis of the original building. The duo brought in top designer Francesc Pons to create a Manhattan-style space, decorated in black, hot pink and shimmering copper.

A bar at one end serves genteel flutes of cava to a serious pre-dinner crowd, while the house DJ treads a careful path along modern jazz and retro lounge. But, as the last of the plates are cleared away, the tempo moves up a gear, and the drinks of choice change from bubbly to Cosmopolitans and Martinis.

Such a sleek and chic vibe wouldn't normally bode well for the food, but this is what makes Noti unique. Not only is it wildly fashionable, but it also manages to place equal emphasis on superb cuisine. Ironically, Crespin has no truck with food fads and modish presentation. Yes, classic recipes are given an occasional twist, but never for the sake of phony creativity. Fish soup is fish soup – a sublime, aromatic affair, bursting with flavour. Tuna *tataki* (slices of seared, peppered tuna) is exemplary, and steak medallions cooked with Chinese five-spice and served with a slick of puréed potato is textbook stuff. The pain has been taken out of choosing a dessert with a selection plate containing a tiny morsel of each, but the cheeseboard is also too good to miss. **Expensive**

Shibui *top-flight Japanese* `1 C4`
C/Comte d'Urgell 272–4 • 93 321 9004
Open lunch & dinner Mon–Sat

Industrial-grey cardboard walls (made from the same material as the menus), Japanese plastic place mats, vases of giant bamboo, pebble gardens and a blonde wood bar reigned over by knife-wielding sushi chefs combine to set the tone of this Tokyo-inspired restaurant. Smart, sassy and gargantuan by Barcelona standards, Shibui spreads out over two floors, including a basement level that's equipped with knee-high *kotatsu* tables (ideal for parties).

The sushi bar is the natural heart of the place, however, and a haven for lone diners. It serves more than 100 variations of beautifully presented sushi and sashimi. The restaurant's top dishes include stingingly spicy tuna rolls and *tataki umaki* – a splendid arrangement of shrimp tempura wrapped in butter-soft, sake-infused rice and topped with a slice of blood-red tuna. **Expensive**

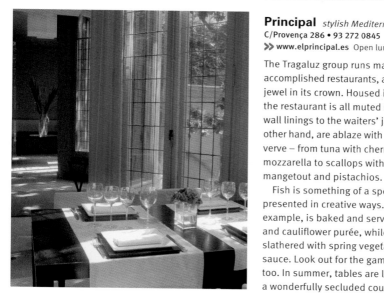

Principal *stylish Mediterranean cuisine* `1 D4`
C/Provença 286 • 93 272 0845
>> www.elprincipal.es Open lunch & dinner daily

The Tragaluz group runs many of Barcelona's most accomplished restaurants, and Principal is the elegant jewel in its crown. Housed in a Modernista mansion, the restaurant is all muted shades of grey, from the wall linings to the waiters' jackets. The dishes, on the other hand, are ablaze with Mediterranean colour and verve – from tuna with cherry tomatoes, avocado and mozzarella to scallops with white truffle, shredded mangetout and pistachios.

Fish is something of a speciality here, and is presented in creative ways. Wild sea bass, for example, is baked and served with wild mushrooms and cauliflower purée, while monkfish comes slathered with spring vegetables, clams and saffron sauce. Look out for the game dishes when in season, too. In summer, tables are laid out under the trees in a wonderfully secluded courtyard. **Expensive**

>> *For advice about tipping,* see p23

Moo *fine wines and food in a sleek setting*   `1 D4`
C/Rosselló 265 • 93 445 400
≫ www.hotelomm.es   Open lunch & dinner Mon–Sat

Moo is the latest venture of the esteemed brothers Roca, who have one of Catalunya's best restaurants in Girona, Celler de Can Roca *(see p46)*. Their Barcelona venture is located at the rear of the lobby of the Hotel Omm, and is the epitome of tasteful design – ultra chic, with a glass back wall and bamboo garden.

Moo also has some great personal touches, such as individual sculptures on each table rather than flower arrangements (those are saved for the centre of the room, and are built up in huge, ornamental structures). The encyclopedic wine list pictures the wine makers themselves alongside detailed descriptions of each wine. The sommeliers at Moo

are among the best trained in Barcelona – real-life Bacchuses despite their tender years.

The food is rich, inventive and served in half-portions, which makes it easy to create your own bespoke menu. Alternatively, opt for the chef's tasting menu, in which each course is paired with a different wine – excellent value at around €85 per head. Depending on the season, expect a host of intriguing titbits, such as eggs and Pedro Jimenez (a stunning creation of sweetly infused onion soup yielding a soft poached egg); Dublin Bay prawns sautéed in Gewürztraminer and Sauvignon blanc, with curry, rose and liquorice; sticky sweet veal cheeks with spices; crunchy, lip-smackingly delicious spiced belly pork; and puddings inspired by perfumes and fruit to brighten jaded palates. Clever stuff. **Expensive**

Ot *creative Mediterranean*

2 H3

C/Còrsega 537 • 93 435 8048
>> www.otrestaurant.net
Open lunch & dinner Mon–Fri, dinner only Sat

Honey-hued Ot in many ways pioneered the new restaurant scene in Barcelona. Opened in 1996, it hit the ground running, chef Ferran Caparrós dazzling diners with hitherto unheard-of creations (unless you were among the few who ate at El Bulli, *see p47*). Though it is perhaps less tremulously exciting in these heady days, when pre-starter *amuse-bouches* and wacky dishes have become commonplace, Ot continues to deliver smart, satisfying, sassy food.

The eight-course tasting menu is a set selection, offering market-fresh ingredients, fashioned into creative treats. You might expect turbot in an Asian-style broth of coconut, shiitake mushrooms and basil; or wild boar with violet potatoes and chocolate *alioli* (mayonnaise dip); dessert may feature a combination of curry and cardamom ice cream. **Expensive**

Chido One *regional Mexican*

2 F2

C/Torrijos 30 • 93 285 0335
Open lunch & dinner daily

This groovy but authentic Mexican restaurant in the heart of Gràcia offers a great range of specialities. Try a heart-warming *posole* (white maize stew), a genuine red or green chilli, and sides of mashed corn and black bean fritters. Quench your thirst with one of the refreshing *aguas frescas* in tropical flavours. **Cheap**

L'Illa de Gràcia *no-frills vegetarian*

2 E3

C/Sant Domènec 19 • 93 238 0229
Open lunch & dinner Tue–Sun

This was one of the first vegetarian restaurants in the city, and it stands out for its plain, natural wood finish rather than opting for the more usual "Earth Mother" environment. It is good for dishes such as veggie crepes, spinach tarts, mushroom risottos and healthy desserts of the muesli-soya-carob bent. **Cheap**

Flash Flash *fifty types of tortilla*

1 D2

C/Granada del Penedès 25 • 93 237 0990
Open lunch & dinner daily

This unusual concept restaurant – decorated with Twiggy-esque silhouettes – is the work of famed Catalan photographer Leopoldo Pomés. An equally stylish clientele come to feast on tortillas of every imaginable flavour (including some dessert specialities) and some of the best burgers in town. **Cheap**

Restaurants

Laurak *modern Basque style* `1 D2`

C/Granada del Penedès 14–16 • 93 218 7165
>> www.laurak.net
Open lunch & dinner Wed–Sat, lunch only Mon & Tue

The design of this excellent Basque restaurant is very striking, as the wooden slats of the understated façade segue into a cruise-ship-style corridor and bar inside. The dining room is a pale blue, its coolness contrasting with the frenetic open kitchen at one end.

The cornerstones of Basque cuisine are all present and correct: *cod a la vizcaína* (with sweet dried red peppers, onions and ham); clams in a white wine and parsley sauce; and fish of the day with garlic and sautéed potatoes. However, they sit alongside such creative offerings as duck liver with banana caramel and diced mango, and Idiazabal cheese mousse with quince steamed in cider. Two tasting menus are available – an avant-garde gourmet selection, or a simpler traditional one. You'll need to book at lunch time, but evenings are often quiet. **Expensive**

Botafumeiro *vast seafood barn* `2 E2`

C/Gran de Gràcia 81 • 93 218 4230
>> www.botafumeiro.es Open lunch & dinner daily

The biggest and best fish restaurant in the city can seem a little daunting at first. Yet, despite the vast size of Botafumeiro, service manages to be personal and the atmosphere is intimate. Every fish you can think of and more is on offer – baked, fried, steamed or grilled, and served in myriad ways. **Expensive**

Breakfast in Barcelona

A typical Barcelona breakfast is little more than a short, strong coffee – a *cortado* – accompanied by a croissant, a *montadito* (small sandwich), or a cake of some kind – sometimes washed down with a glass of red wine. For something more, and especially for the sweet-toothed, few places beat **Escribà** (Las Ramblas 83; Map 5 C3) in terms of atmosphere and melt-in-the-mouth pastries and cakes. **Dos Trece** (C/Carme 40; Map 5 B2) does a Mexican style weekend brunch of *huevos rancheros* (tortillas, eggs and a spicy, tomato sauce) and potent Bloody Marys. By contrast to family-friendly Dos Trece, **La Fianna** (C/Banys Vells 15; Map 6 F4) is the haunt of night owls who can't face the morning sun. Eggs florentine and steak sandwiches are the order of the day here.

Can Travi Nou *robust Catalan fare*

C/Jorge Manrique s/n • 93 428 0301 • Montbau metro
>> www.gruptravi.com
Open lunch & dinner Mon–Fri, dinner only Sat

Housed in a lovingly restored 17th-century *masia* (farmhouse), Can Travi Nou harks back to the days before the urban sprawl reached the upper barrios. It is a trek to get to, but worth it for the old-world atmosphere of its rambling gardens, sprawling terraces, and dining rooms stuffed with old farming tools and antiques worn smooth with age. Because of its size, this is a good place to go in a group and a fabulous place to kick back over a long, lazy Sunday lunch.

Prices are a little high for the robust fare it mostly deals in – dishes of roasted and char-grilled meats, as well as fresh fish – but the restaurant does offer some luxury dishes too. Among the more sophisticated items on the menu are lobster on a chickpea purée, sole and salmon roll with crab coulis, and pan-fried *foie (see p31)* with Calvados jelly. **Expensive**

Cardona 7 *inventive tapas*

C/Cardona 7, Vic • 93 886 3815 • Vic station, then walk (5–10mins) Open lunch & dinner Tue–Sat, lunch only Sun

Tired of catering to the elite in the Michelin-starred restaurant that bore his name, Jordi Parramon downsized the business to a buzzing tapas joint. The chef's exacting standards are still in evidence, as are some of his signature dishes – try the pigs' trotters stuffed with Mallorcan *sobrassada* sausage. **Moderate**

Racó de Can Fabes *gourmet temple*

C/Sant Joan 6, Sant Celoni • 93 867 2851 • Sant Celoni station
>> www.canfabes.com Open lunch & dinner Tue–Sat, lunch Sun

The restaurant of chef Santi Santamaria has long been a fixture on the map of travelling gourmets. Many argue that the food is the best in Spain. The repertoire might include melting pigs' trotters matched by salty caviar, and delicate veal carpaccio with anchovies. Well worth the trip if you have deep pockets. **Expensive**

>> *For the essentials of Catalan cuisine,* see p31

Sant Pau *modern Catalan*
C/Nou 10, Sant Pol • 93 760 0662 • Sant Pol station
»» www.ruscalleda.com
Open lunch & dinner Mon, Wed, Fri & Sat, lunch only Sun,
dinner only Thu; closed 3 weeks in May, 3 weeks in Nov

A welcome female face in the virtually all-male pantheon of great Spanish chefs, Carme Ruscalleda is one of the best. She places the emphasis on really fresh local ingredients and, without resorting to gimmicks, leaves diners dazzled, charmed and sated. The setting is equally appealing – on the seafront in the pretty fishing village of Sant Pol. A garden out front provides an ideal spot to sip an apéritif or coffee.

The menu changes monthly, but signature dishes include *espardenyes* (sea cucumbers) with courgette, creamed potato and parsley pesto; veal *cap-i-cua* (head and tail) with spiced vegetables; and a platter of five local cheeses, each paired with a complementary flavour, such as cherry tomato jelly. A winning combination of gastronomy and setting. **Expensive**

Celler de Can Roca *sublime and extraordinary*
Carretera Taialà 40 • 972 222 157 • Girona station, then taxi
»» www.elcellerdecanroca.com
Open lunch & dinner Tue–Sat; closed 2 weeks in Jul

When the three Roca brothers (chef Joan, pastry chef Jordi and Josep the maître d') took over their parents' bar, it cannot have occurred to them that years later it would be one of Europe's finest restaurants. If it had, they would perhaps have switched location. Stuck out in an unprepossessing suburb of Girona, Celler de Can Roca gives no hint from the outside of the superlative dining experience that awaits within.

It is possible to eat regally à la carte, but it would be a pity not to sample one of the tasting menus. This is thrilling stuff, from the fig compote with a "soup" of foie gras to a scoop of wild mushroom ice cream in a spun sugar globe containing a puff of wood smoke! Desserts are equally extraordinary, and Can Roca's wine cellar is one of the most extensive in the country. Reserve well in advance. **Expensive**

El Bulli *the world's most talked-about restaurant*

Cala Montjoi, Roses • 34 972 150 457 • Figueres, then taxi
➤➤ www.elbulli.com
Open Apr–Jun: dinner Wed–Sun; Jul–Sep: dinner daily

If you eat at just one more restaurant in your lifetime, make it El Bulli – the restaurant that changed the foodie world. Not everybody agrees with Ferran Adrià's approach to cooking; many argue that he's gone too far with experimentation, producing dishes that you'd hardly recognize as a meal. However, there is no doubt that dinner at this rather humble-looking seaside cottage will change the way you look at – and, of course, taste – food forever.

Dinner starts at 8pm and lasts for at least four hours. It is whatever the master and his troop of sous-chefs have hit upon that day (the results of months spent in a secret Barcelona laboratory in the closed season).

There are 33 courses in total, all of them surprising, delightful, mysterious, frightening, bold and usually mesmerizingly beautiful.

It is impossible to predict what you might encounter, but blasts from the past include a Mojito cocktail that is mixed and frozen at the table using liquid nitrogen; deconstructed paella that comes in the form of crisped rice in a paper bag; a balloon of orange-blossom perfumed air, which is popped and inhaled as a precursor to a spoonful of Seville orange sorbet; and a wafer-thin slice of fried milk, sprinkled with Sichuan flower pollen, which causes the tongue to tingle and salivate wildly.

Whichever way you look at it, all this plus four fabulous wines for around €150 is a bargain that would be impossible elsewhere. Booking several months in advance is crucial. **Expensive**

➤➤ *In 2005 Sant Pau was awarded three Michelin stars, putting it alongside El Bulli and Racó de Can Fabes (p45)*

shopping

Barcelona crams an amazingly diverse range of shops into its compact centre. From the souvenir stalls of the Ramblas to the quaint antiques shops of the Barri Gòtic, from funky streetwear outlets in the Raval to the cutting-edge design showrooms of the Born, from chi-chi designer labels on the Passeig de Gràcia to old-school grocery stores of the Eixample, every option offers a unique and atmospheric experience.

SHOPPING

There are two things that are very important to Catalans – looking good and eating well – and visitors can reap the benefits of their exacting demands by shopping at some of the most exciting and enticing stores in Europe. Barcelonins' exacting tastes are catered to by specialist shops that provide only the best in fashion, jewellery, homewares and tasty treats such as cheese, charcuterie and wine. The only problem is fitting into the latest designs after taking advantage of the gastronomic delights.

Kirsten Foster

Food and Drink

There's a shop for every course in Barcelona: artisan charcuterie from **La Botifarreria de Santa Maria** *(see p62)* can provide starters and mains, the farmhouse cheeses at **Formatgeria La Seu** *(see p52)* are perfect for dessert. Wash it all down with fine wine from **Vila Viniteca** *(see p64)*, and for after-dinner coffee and chocolates visit **Casa Gispert** *(see p62)*.

Catalan Culture

Want to buy your way into Catalan society? First, get kitted out with traditional espadrilles from **Manual Alpargatera** *(see p53)* and dress up in a fantastical costume from **El Ingenio** *(see p54)* for one of the many local festivals. Complete the disguise by supping *horchata* (tiger nut milk) or nibbling a bar of *turrón* from **Planelles Donat** *(see p60)*.

Design for Life

Barcelona has long been known as the city of design. **Caixa de Fang** *(see p52)* is the place for colourfully painted earthenware, used in local kitchens for generations. Contrast it in your own home with one of **Recdi8**'s *(see p62)* playful pieces of cutting-edge design, or a high-tech kitchen gadget from design department store **Vinçon** *(see p71)*.

choice shops

High Fashion

Barcelona takes fashion seriously – an art form no less – so don't be surprised if you find yourself taking in an exhibition while browsing the creations at shop-cum-gallery **La Gauche Divine** *(see p54)*. But fashion can be fun too, with **Custo's** *(see p62)* colourful T-shirts and **Giménez y Zuazo's** *(see p64)* clothes with prints derived from playground culture.

Comfy, Sexy and Hip Footwear

Spain is the birthplace of **Camper** *(see p67)*, so it's little wonder that Barcelona is the best place to try its quirky range of "shoes with soul". For those who prefer elegance to eco, **Fior di Loto** *(see p63)* has the sleekest Italian designs. **Kwatra** *(see p64)*, on the other hand, showcases the hippest in limited-edition sports footwear.

Stylish Accessories

There are myriad specialist accessories shops in the city. Some, such as **Alonso** *(see p56)*, have been adding the perfect finish to Catalan ladies' outfits for over 100 years. **L'Arca de l'Avia's** *(see p55)* antique shawls inspired the costume designer on the film *Titanic*. For more up-to-date designs visit jewellery-store-cum-gallery **Hipotesi** *(see p71)*.

Shopping

Caixa de Fang *traditional ceramics* `6 E3`
C/Freneria 1, off C/Llibreteria • 93 315 1704
Open 10–8 Mon–Sat

The *fang* in the name means clay – the raw material for the colourful traditional ceramics that are the hallmark of this compact shop. Items such as *crema catalana* dishes (like ramekins), olive wood pestles and mortars, and rustic casserole dishes are as beautiful as they are useful in the kitchen.

Papirum *luxurious stationery* `6 E3`
Baixada Llibreteria 2 • 93 310 5242
>> www.papirum-bcn.com
Open 10–8:30 Mon–Fri, 10–2 & 5–8:30 Sat

This tiny, atmospheric shop is filled with exquisite marbled fountain pens, handmade paper in delicate shades and leather-bound diaries and notepads. If you're looking for a gift, you can get it all here – present, wrapping paper, card and pen!

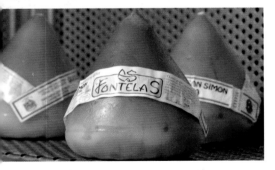

Formatgeria La Seu *quality cheeses* `6 E3`
C/Dagueria 16 • 93 412 6548
>> www.formatgerialaseu.com Open 10–2 & 5–8 Tue–Sat

Set in a former butter-making dairy, this shop sells cheeses from all over Spain, including the smoky, breast-shaped San Simon from Galicia. The friendly, enthusiastic owner, Scotswoman Katherine McLaughlin, also offers tastings of three cheeses with wine for a few euros (noon–2 & 5–8 Tue–Sat).

Papabubble *handmade humbugs* `6 E5`
C/Ample 28 • 93 268 8625
>> www.papabubble.com Open 10–2 & 4–8:30
Tue–Fri, 10–8:30 Sat, 11–7:30 Sun; closed Aug

Despite its 19th-century air and old-fashioned display cabinets, Papabubble is a new shop, staffed by cool young things. Long snakes of handmade candy – in flavours ranging from citrus fruits to fragrant lavender – are snipped into suckable lumps before your eyes.

Carrer d'Avinyó *cool clothes & homewares* `5 D4`

This winding street, off C/Ferran, has an artistic, bohemian history that is reflected in its shops and ambience. As a young man, Picasso studied at the art school that still stands here, and today's arty types come to find decorative touches for their homes and themselves. Students love **Produit National Brut** (No. 29) for its sweat tops emblazoned with the names of Barcelona's cool neighbourhoods, such as Barrio Chino. The shop also stocks second-hand fashions and kitsch retro knick-knacks.

Style aficionados love the range of art and design books and magazines at **Dom** (No. 7). This funky homewares store stocks conversation-starting pieces, such as battery-operated portable turntables and Austin-Powers-style bubble chairs. Top designer labels (Vivienne Westwood, Gaultier, et al) can be found at **Loft Avignon** (No. 22), while even more exclusive labels, such as Yamamoto and Sessun, hang in **So_da** (No. 24), an achingly hip shop that turns into a bar at night. **Angel Gimeno** at No. 25 is just for guys, with clothes for the street or the club by Energie, D&G and Calvin Klein.

It's not all cutting-edge modernity round here, though. A sense of history lingers in the traditional wares sold at **Manual Alpargatera** (No. 7), a vendor of handmade traditional espadrilles since 1910. Designs range from the wedge-heeled, ankle-tied style (a surprise hit of recent years) to the traditional shoe worn by dancers of the local folk jig, the *sardana*. The shop even made a pair for Pope John Paul II. **Sombreria Obach** on the corner of Avinyó with C/Call is another great old classic. Its windows are filled with hats of all kinds – from mohair berets to traditional Catalan caps (which look like red pixie hats), as well as a fine selection of trilbies, fedoras and stetsons.

La Gauche Divine *fashion and art* `5 C5`
Passatge de la Pau 7 • 93 301 6125
≫ www.lagauchedivine.com Open 11–2:30 & 5–8:30 Mon–Sat

Bored with the simple money-for-goods exchange of traditional shopping? Here you can do so much more – take in an exhibition, watch a video or listen to a DJ set. The normal aspects of shopping are not entirely absent, of course, and you can also try and buy clothes by hot young Barcelona designers such as Txell Miras.

Herboristeria del Rei *herbal wonders* `5 C3`
C/Vidre 1 • 93 318 0512
≫ www.herboristeriadelrei.com
Open 5–8 Mon, 10–2 & 5–8 Tue–Sat

This herbalist store has been around since the 1820s and boasts a stunning interior. Its ornate shelves are piled with painted ceramic jars and glass phials, and its wooden drawers are full of herbs, spices and infusions for medicinal, cosmetic and culinary usage.

El Ingenio *big heads and little tricks* `5 D3`
C/Rauric 6 • 93 317 7138
≫ www.el-ingenio.com
Open 10–1:30 & 4:45–8 Mon–Fri, 10–2 & 5:15–8:30 Sat

The historic El Ingenio has old glass cabinets filled with schoolboy tricks, juggling clubs and unusual toys. Look up and you'll come face to face with fantastic oversize heads and grimacing masks – the costumes of Carnaval and the mad Mercè festival *(see p18)*.

Caelum *tasty gifts* `5 D2`
C/Palla 8 • 93 302 6993 Open 5:30–8:30 Mon, 10:30–8:30 Tue–Thu, 10:30–9:30 Fri & Sat ✓

A shop-cum-café, Caelum sells traditional cakes, preserves and other foodstuffs, as well as wines and spirits. What's exceptional here, though, is that all the products are made by monks and nuns in cloistered orders. You can take your purchases away or consume them in the arcaded downstairs dining room.

Carrer Banys Nous *history for sale* `5 D3`

Lovers of all things old and antiquated will find plenty to tempt them on this atmospheric lane off C/Ferran. Memorabilia collectors should direct themselves to the antique adverts and postcards in **Colleccionisme Coixet** (No. 19), while **L'Arca de L'Avia** (No. 20) and **Heritage** (No. 14) are cluttered treasure chests of antique silk, linens and lace. The kimonos sold in Japanese textiles shop **Nunoya** (No. 20) may not be antique, but the silk ceremonial versions are certainly works of art. Toy shop **Joquines Foyé** (No. 13) updates an old idea with a range of clockwork tin toys in the shape of Simpsons characters. Old also meets new in **Café La Granja** (No. 4), a revamped historic café, with an original Roman wall, Modernista frontage and a funky young vibe. Weary shoppers should try the chilli hot chocolate for a buzz. Close by, **Gemma Povo** (No. 7; www.gemmapovo.com) sells elegant wrought-iron furniture, and **Germanes Garcia** at No. 15 offers wickerwork baskets, chairs, lamp shades and shelves.

Drap *stylish homewares – for little people!* `5 D2`
C/Pi 14 • 93 318 1487
>> www.ample24.com/drap
Open 10–1:30 & 4:30–8:30 Mon–Fri, 10–1:30 & 5–8:45 Sat

The enthusiastic staff at Drap take pride in each item they sell, from finely crafted dolls' houses to all of the paraphernalia that goes inside – mini saucepans, tiny oventops, even miniature toilets! If you've ever wanted to feel like a giant, this is the place to go.

Xocoa *designer chocolates in cool packaging* `5 D2`
C/Petritxol 11–13 • 93 301 1197
>> www.xocoa-bcn.com Open 9–9 daily (closed 2–4 Sun)

With chocolate bars enhanced by the flavours of any-thing from rosemary to raspberries, and unique delicacies such as *ventalls* (truffle-filled sponges), even the most ardent chocoholic should be satiated here. The chocolate theme continues with cocoa candles and T-shirts emblazoned with "I'm bitter".

>> *If you are using a credit card to shop, remember to carry your passport, which you will need to show as ID*

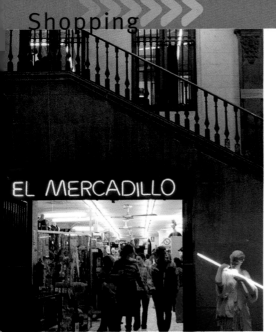

El Mercadillo *club clothes & retro glamour* 5 D2

C/Portaferrissa 17 • 93 301 8913
Open 11–9 Mon–Sat

You'll recognize El Mercadillo by the giant fibreglass camel that guards the entrance to this rambling "market" of second-hand and club-style gear on one of Barcelona's top shopping streets. The ground floor caters for skate kids and podium dancers, with stalls such as **LXR** providing everything for the slopes or the half-pipe – from shades to baggy pants to boards. **Invasion** sells the popular culture *artefact du jour* – Mexican wrestling masks. By contrast, **Eligene's** racks are filled with Lycra-and-lace creations that are tailor-made for the heat of the dance floor.

Head to the back of the market and up the stairs to find a hidden terrace café. This oasis from the bustle of the stalls and shops below is a favourite with local students, who flirt, gossip and cast a critical eye over each other's fashions while sipping Mojitos and sharing plates of cheese and charcuterie.

Alonso *elegant accessories* 5 D1

C/Santa Anna 27 • 93 317 6085
≫ www.tiendacenter.com Open 10–8 Mon–Sat

The Alonso family has run this *complementes* store since 1905. The display windows are crammed with the full range of their stock, including fancy lace and soft leather gloves, and scarves of embroidered silk. An enormous assortment of fans includes modern designs influenced by the work of Joan Miró.

Casas *footwear with flair* 5 D1

Rambla Canaletes (Las Ramblas) 125 • 93 302 4598
≫ www.casasclub.com Open 10–8:30 Mon–Sat

This small Ramblas store offers the cream of Spanish shoe design. Women can choose from Chie Mihara's sexy range of tango shoes and Dorotea's felt wedges in brash, childlike colours. The men are offered more restrained brogues and loafers by Yanko. Branch U-Casas (C/Tallers 2) has the latest trainers.

Galerias Malda *mini mall* `5 D2`
C/Portaferrissa 22/C/Pi 5

There's something for everyone at Barcelona's oldest shopping mall in the centre of the Barri Gòtic, but the smallest members of the family are those best catered for. Little angels can be made to look even cuter in fluffy romper suits from **Els Angels** (A6). But they could show their devilish side if you try dragging them away from the hundreds of stuffed toys at **Birimbola** (A4). Their bigger brothers may be more impressed by the sharp clothes at **Aragaza** (A28; www.aragaza.com) – figure-hugging shirts fashioned in red silk or crisp white cotton.

   Platamundi (A40; www.platamundi.com) manages to make you feel angelic while spoiling yourself. When you buy a piece from their modern jewellery collection, 1% of the money goes to development projects in Togo. And while you're treating yourself for being so very good, why not indulge further, with some heavenly bath soaps from the "shop of smells", **Magistral** (C3).

Arlequi Mascares *masks and puppets* `6 F3`
C/Princesa 7 • 93 268 2752
>> www.arlequimask.com
Open 10:30–8:30 Mon–Sat, 10:30–4:30 Sun

With its beautifully crafted masks, Arlequi is the city's temple to the masquerade. A half-face creation will cost from €20 to over €200, but you are welcome simply to browse their amazing collection of Catalan, Comedia dell'Arte, Noh theatre and other masks.

Fashion Chains

Zara (Passeig de Gràcia 16; www.zara.com) is trend-savvy, bringing catwalk looks to the high street for men and women. **Mango** (Passeig de Gràcia 65; www.mango.es) is aimed at the more mature woman, with stylish separates that can adapt to the boardroom or bar. Prices in both are much lower here than abroad. **Women's Secret** (C/Portaferrissa 7; www.womensecret.com) sells lingerie, underwear and swimwear. Its designs range from cuddly to sexy, and are always comfortable.

   The bold claim of **Desigual** (C/Argenteria 65; www.desigual.com) is that "it is not the same". And, indeed, this brash, street-fashion chain certainly is not, judging by the highly visible adverts which feature naked people rather than the shop's clothes.

>> *Zara and Mango also have outlets on Portal de l'Angel, see p60*

Portal de l'Angel *high-street shopping* `5 D1`

Leading away from Plaça de Catalunya and running parallel with Las Ramblas, this pedestrianized avenue is Barcelona's "high street". Most shoppers home in on clothing giants **Zara** and **Mango** *(see p57)* for excellent ranges of street-smart fashion at bargain prices. However, there are many independent stores still holding their own against the encroaching giants. **Rafa** (No. 3) has the best in bags, stocking prized labels such as Mandarina Duck and Lamarthe. If you haven't yet tried *turrón* (a marzipan-like sweet from Valencia), **Planelles Donat** (No. 7) is the place to do so. As well as great *turrón*, the shop also sells fine ice cream, and its parlour at No. 25 is the locals' favourite.

Ciutad (No. 14) has been here since 1882, and its wares are like relics from a more elegant age. Translucent, amber-coloured tortoiseshell combs, glistening vanity sets and natural bristle brushes are arranged with reverence, as if they were important medical instruments. Another blast from the past, haberdashery **Merceria Santa Ana** (No. 26; www.merceriasantaana.com) is an always-bustling mini-mart for everything you can make and wear, from brides' garters to babies' booties. The purchasing system is as antiquated as the store – you go to one desk to place your order, another to pay, then back again to pick up your goods. But relax, and see it as a chance to chat and mingle with the locals.

Carrer de l'Argenteria *sharp style* **6 F4**

This pedestrianized thoroughfare is the gateway to the trendy Born area, and its mix of quality shops is a microcosm of what's on offer elsewhere in Barcelona's hippest neighbourhood. The road is particularly good for modern jewellery. **Ona Joia** (No. 25; www.onajoia. com) has an extensive collection, and includes Andrea Blú's dogtag-style chains for men. **Alea** (No. 66) is a jewellery gallery – the long glass cases at the front are dedicated solely to Enric Majoral's structural pieces of interwoven silver and gold. The small space at the rear of the shop showcases the work of various young designers, their pieces as much art as accessories.

For more affordable baubles, **Bijou Brigitte** (No. 6) has everything from chunky diamanté rings to trendy plastic bangles. The stock at **Opera Prima** (No. 45) has more of a retro feel, with Les Néréides' Art Deco-like diamanté necklaces, and hats and bags in velvet, lace and sequins. Next door, **Como Agua de Mayo** (No. 43) stocks inventive clothes by young Spanish designers – check out Mariona Gen's quirky jumpers, which have prints of faces peering through woollen frames. **La Sabateria del Born's** (No. 41) funky range of shoes shows clear gender distinction: Lollipop's girly slip-ons with dolly decorations for women; Rankin's butch, square-toed and studded lace-ups for men.

Even the non-fashion stores here are stylish. Specialist coffee roaster **Cafes El Magnifico** (No. 64; www.cafeselmagnifico.com) blends Modernista and modern architecture in its fragrant store, where each cru, or regional variety, of coffee is treated respectfully. Its sister shop, **Sans & Sans** (No. 59), has a Zen-like interior – a fitting setting for the stock of over 300 teas, and exquisite Chinese and Japanese tea sets.

Shopping

Recdi8 *quirky gifts and homewares* `6 F4`
C/Espaseria 20 • 93 268 0257
>> www.recdi8.com Open 5–8:30 Mon,
11:30–2:30 & 5–8:30 Tue–Fri, noon–2 & 5–9 Sat

Barcelona is full of shops selling gimmicky things for the home. Recdi8's stock is similar in kind but far better in quality – hand-picked items are produced by top design houses, as evident in Progetti's update of the cuckoo clock and cool Plexiglas barcode watches.

La Botifarreria de Santa Maria `6 F4`
C/Santa Maria 4 • 93 319 9784
Open 8:30–2:30 & 5–8:30 Mon–Fri, 8:30–3 Sat

Handmade *botifarra* sausages, created at the back of the store, are the top draw to this cheese and cured meat specialist. *Botifarras* are a traditional staple of the Catalan diet, but the owner conjures up original creations too, mixing pork with ingredients such as squid and curry. The shop is closed in August.

Casa Gispert *master roasters* `6 F4`
C/Sombrerers 23 • 93 319 7535
>> www.casagispert.com

Open 9:30–2 & 4–7:30 Mon–Fri, 10–2 & 5–8 Sat

Casa Gispert started in 1851, selling coffee, tea, cocoa, spices and saffron from the Americas. Today the family has added speciality oils, vinegars, preserves and chocolates to the repertoire, as well as delicious nuts, roasted in the shop's original wood-fired oven.

Custo *colourful clothing* `6 F4`
Plaça de les Olles 7 • 93 268 7893
>> www.custo-barcelona.com Open 10–9 Mon–Sat, noon–8 Sun

The Catalan Dalmau brothers' bright, brash T-shirts were first seen in the 1980s in LA, where stars such as Julia Roberts snapped them up. Today, the company's trademark cut-and-paste designs, fusing illustration, embroidery, patchwork and graphic elements, can also be seen on jeans, dresses and jackets.

Czar *hip glamour for feet* `6 F4`
Passeig del Born 20 • 93 310 7222
Open 4–9 Mon, 11–2 & 4–9 Tue–Sat

A tiny shop, dedicated to seeking out and selling the hippest footwear. Adidas Originals special editions are presented like cultural artifacts. Vision Streetwear's offerings include leopard-fur skate shoes. The small, well-chosen women's range includes sassy but smart pointed flats from Killah.

---

62   ✓ *Good value*   For the very latest on Barcelona go to >> **www.realcity.dk.com**

Carrer dels Flassaders *boutique chic* `6 G4`

This atmospheric cobbled alleyway between C/Princesa and Passeig del Born is lined with medieval vaulted warehouses that have been converted into curious craft shops, cutting-edge design showrooms and food shops.

Delectable aromas waft from the Italian deli **BoccaBacco** (www.boccabacco.com) at No. 44; buy one of its vegetable tarts, redolent with Mediterranean herbs, and a slice of rich, velvety tiramisu for an instant picnic. The Italian invasion continues a few doors down at No. 31, where **Fior di Loto** stocks elegant, Italian-made footwear. The high heels and pointed toes in glamorous animal prints and glitter are mainly from the shop's own label, though it does also stock other brands, including Nina's fun, colourful wellies.

Kaveh Abadani (www.kavehabadani.com) at No. 32 sells sculptural "bodywear" – jewellery, quirky hair clips and candy-coloured bangles – as well as lamps, amazing floral wall lights and an array of home furnishing accessories. They are all the designs of the owner Kaveh Abadani, a young prize-winning Iranian designer who studied in London. Abadani uses traditional techniques for weaving but employs unusual materials such as wire and plastic resin, inspiration coming from his cultural background.

Elisa Brunells (www.elisabrunells.com) at Nos 36–8 is a young Catalan designer specializing in jewellery. In her shop you'll find exquisite small pieces for body decoration, each item handmade in silver to original modern designs, and each a unique artistic creation.

Giménez y Zuazo *playful urban fashion* `5 C1`
C/Elisabets 20 • 93 412 33 81
>> www.gimenezzuazo.com Open 10:30–2:30, 5–8:30 Mon–Sat

There's a youthful air to the clothes from this pair of Spanish designers, and not just because of their penchant for material printed with storybook illustrations. The range for women uses quite sober silhouettes, in fact, but is enlivened with cheery embroidery, patchwork or playgroup-friendly colours.

Vila Viniteca *dedicated to wine* `6 E4`
C/Agullers 7 • 93 268 32 27
>> www.vilaviniteca.es
Open 8:30–2.30 & 4:30–8.30 Mon–Fri, 8:30–2:30 Sat

This cathedral to the grape is particularly strong on Catalan wine. Look for reds from the Priorat region, such as the excellent-value Font de la Figuera. For even more of a steal, the silky Gotim Bru, from the Costers del Segre region, is an absolute bargain.

Iguapop *radical art works* `5 C2`
C/Comerç 15 • 93 310 0735
>> www.iguapop.net
Open 5–9 Mon, 11–2:30 & 5–9 Tue–Sat

Showcasing work ignored by mainstream galleries, Iguapop features artists such as cult graffiti artist Boris Hoppek. If you can't afford a piece from the gallery (anything from a few hundred euros upwards), you could always pick up a postcard, book or T-shirt.

Kwatra *limited edition Nikes* `6 G4`
C/Antic de Sant Joan 1 • 93 268 0804
>> www.kwatra.com Open 11–2 & 4–9 Mon–Sat

If you have a Nike addiction, here is your friendly dealer. An ex-Nike employee set up this store to sell the most exclusive and hard-to-find Nike products, such as bags, watches, clothes and, most importantly, sports shoes. Recently stocked limited editions include the Metro Classic, the Oceania and the Cheyenne.

CD Drome *leftfield record store* `4 E1`
C/Valldoncella 3 • 93 317 4646
>> www.cddrome.com
Open 10:30–8:30 Mon–Fri, 10:30–2 & 4:30–8:30 Sat

CD Drome oozes hip. The CD and vinyl stock covers the latest and best in genres such as minimal beats, hands-up vinyl, post-rock and techno. There are decks for trying before you buy, and the store is also great for picking up flyers, listings magazines and tickets.

Carrer dels Tallers *music and fashion* `5 C1`

Tallers means "workshops", in this case the butchers' shops which were sited along this street in the Middle Ages. Appropriately enough, one of the first stores you come to is **Arantxa** (No. 5), a friendly deli-restaurant that specializes in the finest hams and sausages produced in Spain.

These days, though, the street is more musical than meaty. It has several record stores, most of which are branches of **Discos Castello** (www.discoscastello.com). The classical branch is at No. 3; its pop-rock shop at No. 7; hip-hop and alternative are combined at No. 9; and its jazz outlet is at No. 79. The hip kids who come to hang out in the record stores also tend to love the choice of vintage clothing in second-hand store **Holala** (www.holala-ibiza.com) at No. 73. Alongside staples such as camouflage trousers, there are rarer pieces, such as replica Okinawa silk jackets. Last of all, if you are in the mood for a hand-rolled Havana, stop by the fine cigar and pipe shop **Estanc Mesequino** (No. 42).

Riera Baixa *vintage clothes and sounds* `5 B2`

Cutting between C/Carme and C/Hospital, Riera Baixa is the street where those in the know come for inspiration from the best of the past. The leader of the pack is **Lailo** (No. 20), a vintage clothing store that's a major reference point on the fashion scene. It even has a special "museum" of costumes from the local Liceu theatre. On the main shop floor you can find anything from 1950s bathing suits to 1920s coming-out gowns. Everything can be hired as well as bought.

Smart And Clean (No. 7; www.smartandclean.com) has a huge range of choice vintage gear, including original 1970s sports shoes. What Lailo is to the world of fashion, **Discos Edison's** (www.discos-edisons.com) is to the world of vinyl. The store at No. 10 is where you can replace your scratched Kool and the Gang or Blondie album at a good price. It also features more collectable vinyl, from flamenco greats to retro soundtracks and import Beatles albums.

Shopping

Altaïr *travel books, maps and more* 3 D1

Gran Via de les Corts Catalanes 616 • 93 342 7171
>> www.altair.es Open 10–2 & 4:30–8:30 Mon–Sat

The biggest travel bookshop in Europe, Altaïr likes to promote the cultural side of travel, with books on international cuisine and religions, as well as world music CDs. Of course, there are the general travel guides too and everything you could want to prepare for a trip, from maps to a travel information service.

Torres *great value wines* 5 A4
C/Nou de la Rambla 25 • 93 317 3234
>> www.vinosencasa.com Open 9–2 & 4–9 Mon–Sat ✓

After moving from a rundown grocery store across the street, Torres' friendly owners have stocked the new premises floor to ceiling with quality Spanish wines. They also sell a good variety of international beers and spirits, including 160% proof black absinthe from Mallorca. Despite the move, Torres' prices remain low.

Cinemascope *everything for the film fan* 4 E1
C/La Perla 29 • 93 237 2720
Open 10:30–2 & 5–9 Tue–Sat

A cinephile's home from home, Cinemascope has an interior that's plastered with old film posters – *Gone with the Wind, Casablanca* and modern blockbusters like *Pirates of the Caribbean*. Most are for sale, along with photos of the great screen stars, antique cinema programmes and an eclectic selection of DVDs.

Markets

Barcelona has over 40 food markets, including the famous **Boqueria** on the Ramblas *(see p131)*. But for a more authentic (and cheaper) local experience, visit its mini cousin, **Sant Antoni** (C/Comte d'Urgell; Map 3 D2; 7–2:30 & 5:30–8:30 Mon–Thu & Sat, 7–8:30 Fri). On Sundays stalls selling secondhand books and collectable coins set up instead.

Bric-a-brac hunters may get lucky at the flea market **Els Encants** (C/Dos de Maig, near Sagrada Família; 9–6 Mon, Wed, Fri & Sat), where everything from old books to spanners is hawked. Harder bargaining is needed at the Thursday **antiques market** (10–8) in front of the Cathedral (Map 6 E3); it specializes in an intriguing mix of rosaries, *mantillas* (veils) and all manner of memorabilia relating to Barcelona FC.

Camper *shoes with soul* `4 F1`
C/Pelai 13–37 • 93 302 4124
>> www.camper.es Open 10–10 Mon–Sat

With their quirky designs, hip ecological philosophy, and refreshingly comfortable products, Camper footware has gained a cult following over the last 30 years. Though shoemaking has been in the Mallorca-based Fluxa family for the last four generations, it was in 1975 that the founder's grandson Lorenzo created Camper as it is known today, with his concept of shoes based on "freedom, comfort and creativity". The company may have a down-to-earth outlook, rooted in the rural sensibility of Camper's island home, but that doesn't mean you'll look like a hick or a hippy in their shoes. Far from it – Camper has led the way in groundbreaking design, in its shops as well as its shoes. Stores painted in funky colours display the wares attached to the walls with Velcro. Pick up a pair of their best-selling designs, such as the ecological Wabi model.

FNAC *entertainment superstore* `4 F1`
El Triangle, Plaça Catalunya 4 • 93 344 1800
>> www.fnac.es Open 10–10 Mon–Sat

If you can watch it, read it, listen to it or play it, you'll find it at FNAC. On the ground floor is the city's best magazine department, and – as befits a city with a great tradition in art, design, music and fashion – there's a strong leaning towards visual arts magazines and hip "what's on" guides. It carries a substantial foreign language section for those who can't do without their *Heat* magazine or French *Vogue*. The magazines share space with a café, ticket agency, photo processing counter, travel agency and performance space, where films are shown and musicians do free, short sets to plug their latest albums.

The upper floors are devoted to books (including French-, English- and German-language editions), CDs, DVDs, and audiovisual and IT equipment. There are several branches of FNAC, including one at L'Illa, a shopping mall at 545–57 Avinguda Diagonal.

>> *For more about Barcelona's markets, see* pp130–39

Shopping

El Corte Inglés *trad department store* 4 F1
Plaça de Catalunya 14 • 93 306 3800
>> www.elcorteingles.es Open 10–10 Mon–Sat

This cruise-liner-shaped building is an icon over-looking the shopping hub of the Plaça de Catalunya. If you simply must buy extra-virgin olive oil, a pair of designer shoes, some nail varnish remover and a paella pan all in the same place, this is the shop to combine all your retail needs. Prices are often a little higher than elsewhere, but you are compensated by convenience, multilingual staff (and a translation service), a money-back guarantee, and in-store extras such as gift-wrapping and home delivery.

The lower-ground floor is a hideaway for goods and services hard to find elsewhere – a keycutter, shoe repairer and clock and watch workshop – alongside a supermarket where you can pick up organic rocket and fresh lobster. The Club del Gourmet is where homesick ex-pats can find comfort in British pickles, German beer and Japanese sushi ingredients.

Cacao Sampaka *chocoholic's world* 1 D5
C/Consell de Cent 292 • 93 272 0833
>> www.cacaosampaka.com Open 9:30–9:30 Mon–Sat (Aug: noon–8 Tue–Sat)

Here, chocolate is paired with surprising flavours – filled with anchovy or parmesan, infused with delicate herbs and strident spices, or made with cocoa from a single estate. Stop by the shop's café to try a passion fruit and chocolate drink with a chocolate sausage!

Purificación García *playful label* 2 E5
Passeig de Gràcia 21 • 93 487 7292
>> www.purificaciongarcia.es Open 10–8:30 Mon–Sat

The clothes of this Spanish-Uruguyan designer have appeared in many film and theatre productions. And there is, indeed, something distinctly theatrical about her smart, sharp clothing, which is known for its tactile fabrics and splashes of colour. The brand has also branched out into bags, shoes and eyewear.

Bagués *exclusive, expensive jewellery* `2 E5`
Passeig de Gràcia 41 • 93 216 0173
>> www.bagues.es
Open 10–8:30 Mon–Fri, 10–1:30 & 5–8:30 Sat

The 19th-century Modernista palace Casa Amatller is a suitably grand setting for Bagués' gem-encrusted jewellery. Their Masriera line is a prestigious collection of Art Nouveau jewellery, while the shop's modern collection features a new theme each season.

Colmado Quilez *if you can eat it, it's here* `2 E4`
Rambla de Catalunya 63 • 93 215 2356
Open 9–2 & 4:30–8:30 Mon–Fri, 9–2 Sat

Colmados are traditional grocery stores. This is one of the few surviving in the Eixample district, its shelves stacked high with wines, oils, herbs, tinned game, hams, foie gras and a thousand and one other delights. Look for local treats like *Delicias del Bosque* (preserved fungi in mushroom-shaped bottles).

Bulevard dels Antiquaris *collectibles* `2 E4`
Passeig de Gràcia 55 • 93 215 4499
>> www.bulevarddelsantiquaris.com
Open 9:30–1:30 & 4:30–8:30 Mon–Sat

One of the best, easiest and safest places to shop for antiques in Barcelona, the Bulevard dels Antiquaris is an antiques shopping gallery on the prestigious Passeig de Gràcia. Admirers of local artists Miró and Tàpies should head straight to **March** (No. 42) which specializes in limited-edition prints of the works of these Catalan masters. Like his contemporaries, Miró was influenced by African art, which can be bought at **Raquel Montagut** (No. 11), whether it be a wooden mask from the Ivory Coast or a Nigerian funeral urn. **Cronos** at No. 22 deals in Eastern artifacts, such as Khmer carved wooden figures from Cambodia.

Collectors with smaller wallets or luggage allowances can pick up an antique pocket watch or pen from **Tric Trac** at No. 43. This stall of small things also sells old toys, such as trains and model cars.

Shopping

Bulevard Rosa *a bustling maze*

2 E4

Passeig de Gràcia 55 • 93 215 8331

>> www.bulevardrosa.com Open 10:30–9 Mon–Sat

With more than 100 shops, Bulevard Rosa is a retail addict's paradise. It offers many options for clothes, shoes and accessories, but the bulevard also has its share of unique selling points. **El Taller** (No. 97) is the place to go if you cannot find any jewellery to suit, as it sells everything you need to make your own – chains, fasteners and an enormous selection of plastic, Murano glass, wood and semi-precious stone beads. **Items d'Ho** (Nos. 21–4) is the place to find the gift for someone who has everything – everything, that is, except for a portable, egg-shaped fridge or a cow statuette dressed as a construction worker. **Lisboa** (No. 87) seduces you into dreamland with delicate linens, fluffy bed throws and decadent silks. Equally frivolous but far less expensive is that mini icon of the 70s – a Kojak "who loves ya baby" sugar-free lollipop, available from **Humm** (No. 78).

Mantequeria Ravell *gourmet foodstuffs*

2 F5

C/Aragó 313 • 93 457 5114

>> www.ravell.com Open 10–9 Tue–Sat

The shop's name translates as "buttershop Ravell", but the goods here are much more rarefied and exotic than butter. This super-posh deli is for obsessive gourmets, who won't rest until they've sourced pink Himalayan salt, or an exclusive, naturally carbonated Catalan mineral water – the favourite of Salvador Dalí.

La Central *English-language books*

1 D4

C/Mallorca 237 • 93 487 5018

>> www.lacentral.com

Open 9:30–9:30 Mon–Fri, 10–9 Sat

More than just a bookshop, La Central is a community of book lovers. It has an excellent website, while the shop itself has the city's best selection of English-language books – new and old, fiction and non-fiction, bestsellers and more obscure tomes.

Vinçon *living as art* `2 E4`
Passeig de Gràcia 96 • 93 215 6050
» www.vincon.com Open 10–8:30 Mon–Sat

Design department store Vinçon has been at the vanguard of interior design in Barcelona for 40 years – even its carrier bags have become collectors' items. It is worth a visit for the first-floor furniture department alone, which has ornate Modernista decor and an enchanting patio. (From here you get a free peek at Gaudí's La Pedrera, *see p76*.) Almost everything you could need for the home is here in abundance: from rosewood coat hangers to professional blenders, funky bath mats and wine thermometers.

The important thing to note is that every object sold, down to the humblest spatula, is a piece of top contemporary design. Classics such as the Rabbit corkscrew and Global knives are stocked, alongside newer innovations, like stools made from scooter seats and Bar Code shopping bags, a sleeping sheep neck pillow and lightly scented black toilet paper.

Hipotesi *artistic jewellery* `1 D4`
C/Provença 237 • 93 215 0298
Open 10– 1:30 & 5–8:30 Mon & Sat, 10–8:30 Tue–Fri

Part gallery, part shop, Hipotesi is full of unusual jewellery, fashioned in felt and plastic as well as silver and gold. Designs by old hands such as Ramon Puig Cuyas, head of Barcelona's Massana jewellery school, are mixed with the work of newer stars, like Kathryn Marchbank, who works with wire.

Shopping for High-End Fashions
Moschino's Cheap And Chic range is even cheaper at **Le Shoe** (C/Valencia 254; Map 1 D4; 93 215 0535), a discount designer shoe store. Although the shop is small and stock limited, a visit could be rewarded by a pair of Marc Jacobs kitten heels at half price. **Camisería Pons** (Gran de Gràcia 49; Map 2 E2; 93 217 7292) offers skilfully tailored clothes from top Catalan designers. Lydia Delgado's smart but sensual styles use luxurious materials, while men can choose a colourful tie to pair with a sharp suit by Josep Abril. Signs at the doorway of **Contribuciones y Moda** (C/Riera de Sant Miquel 30; Map 2 E3; 93 218 7140) point to catwalk fashions at high street prices. Labels such as Joseph and Commes des Garçons are heavily discounted.

art &
architecture

Barcelona has long been an inspiration to artists, and provided a formative experience for three of the greatest painters of the last 100 years – Picasso, Miró and Dalí. Many of their finest works can be seen in the city's museums. This is also a city of exceptional architecture. From the medieval charms of the Old City to the fantastic visions of Gaudí, to the work of contemporary architects, Barcelona has a wealth of building styles to enjoy.

ART & ARCHITECTURE

For a city of its size, Barcelona boasts an amazing array of buildings with architectural flair. The best way to enjoy them is to take a walk and discover anew the hidden Gothic cloisters of the Old City and the great Modernista works built in the artistically dynamic period of the late 19th century. Today, the city's museums and galleries are among the most inspiring in Europe, and I am drawn back equally to the ancient treasures of MNAC and to the latest shows of contemporary art at places like CCCB and the CaixaForum.

Daniel Campi

Gothic Gems

The **Catedral de Barcelona** *(see p79)* is a majestic spectacle of soaring columns and Gothic arches, but stylistically it is bettered by **Santa María del Mar** *(see p82)*, built in the mid- to late 14th century. The **Shlomo Ben Adret Synagogue** *(see p79)* is a recent discovery, found while digging out the basement of a 13th-century building.

Important Collections

Take a walk through "1,000 years of Catalan art", from Roman frescoes to paintings by Dalí and Tàpies, at **MNAC** *(see p86)*. For modern art, head to **MACBA** *(see p83)* for work by the Dadaists and their successors. The **Museu Frederic Marès** *(see p79)* presents a highly personal collection, taking you from ancient sculpture to 20th-century painting.

Masters of Modern Art

The legacy of one of Barcelona's most cherished sons is amply displayed at the **Fundació Joan Miró** *(see p87)*, while the **Museu Picasso** *(see p81)* is especially good for Pablo's early period. Art museum or Surrealist theme park? That is the question at the eccentric **Teatre-Museu Dalí** *(see p90)* – a must for fans of the moustached genius.

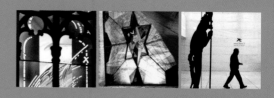

choice sights

Modernista Brilliance

Gaudí's **La Pedrera** *(see p76)* is a symphony in stone and iron, while on the same street **Casa Batlló** *(see p76)* employs a spiralling, deep-sea inspired theme. The dazzling **Palau de la Música Catalana** *(see p98)* is by Domènech i Montaner, often described as Barcelona's "second greatest Modernista". It is now a UNESCO World Heritage Site.

Squares and Cloisters

The oldest church in town, **Esglesia de Sant Pau del Camp** *(see pp84 & 144)*, has a beautiful 12th-century cloister. **Plaça del Rei** *(see p130)* is Barcelona's finest Gothic square, as well as the entrance point for the **Museu d'Història de la Ciutat** *(see p78)*. And in quiet **Plaça Sants Just i Pastor** *(see p142)* you find yourself transported to medieval Barcelona.

Contemporary Exhibition Spaces

The **CaixaForum** *(see p85)* took an old textile factory and turned it into a place to see shows by heavyweights in its main gallery and up-and-coming artists in one of its multiple exhibition spaces. **CCCB** *(see p82)* has a vibrant exhibition programmes and the **Palau de la Virreina** *(see p80)* is particularly good for photography shows.

Art & Architecture

Gaudí's Buildings *Barcelona visionary*

Best known of Spain's Modernista architects *(see p89)*, Gaudí was nevertheless a true original, who created his own architectural language. His break came in 1886, when industrialist Eusebi Güell chose Gaudí to build his family home, **Palau Güell** (Map 5 C4; open 10–8 daily). The interior in particular offers a feast of decorative delights – lavish wooden ceilings, snake-eyed pillars and a plethora of fluid, swirling motifs.

The architect's next major commission was **Casa Milà** (Map 2 E4; open 10–8 daily), also known as **La Pedrera** (the Stone Quarry). The building has an undulating façade that gives the impression of waves. Wrought-iron balconies resembling seaweed continue the oceanic theme, as do the shimmering blue-green walls of the lobby. However, an even more fantastical building stands opposite. **Casa Batlló** (Map 2 E5; www.casabatllo.es; open 9am–8pm daily) was an existing building that Gaudí remodelled, giving full rein to his singular vision. The building is a celebration of creatures, both mythical and real, with elephant-foot columns, a "dragon's back" roof and mosaic tiling reminiscent of glistening reptilian scales.

Gaudí then began work on **Park Güell** (C/Olot; Lesseps metro), which was intended as a "garden city" for an aesthetically minded bourgeoisie. The homes were never built, but what remains is a magical park with twisting paths, avenues of columns intertwined with the natural landscape and a giant mosaic-covered esplanade that overlooks the city.

Gaudí's final project was the **Sagrada Família** (Map 2 H4; www.sagradafamilia.org), a building that has become the emblem of Barcelona. For this vast church, he envisioned 12 towers to represent the Apostles, four domes for the Evangelists and a colossal central spire to honour Christ. Driven by intense religious conviction, Gaudí dedicated himself exclusively to the project from 1908 onwards, even living in the building as a virtual hermit until his death in 1926. To this day, only four towers have been completed, but work continues. A testament to his devotion to the project, Gaudí's body rests in the temple's crypt.

1 Casa Batlló; 2 & 7 Palau Güell; 3, 5 & 8 Casa Milà; 4 Sagrada Família; 6 & 9 Park Güell

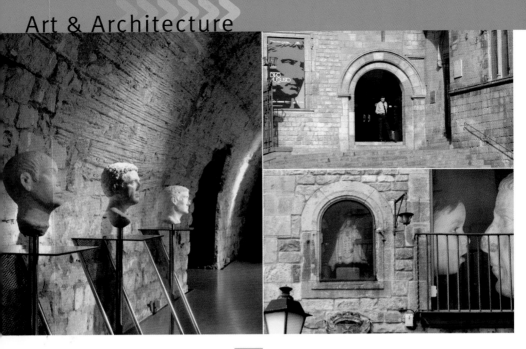

Museu d'Història de la Ciutat

6 E3

Plaça del Rei • 93 315 1111

>> www.museuhistoria.bcn.es Open Jun–Sep: 10–8 Tue–Sat, 10–3 Sun; Oct–May: 10–2 & 4–8 Tue–Sat, 10–3 Sun

Situated in one of Barcelona's most beautiful Gothic squares *(see p130)*, the Museu d'Història de la Ciutat is really a collection of historical buildings and excavations, including the most extensive subterranean Roman ruins in the world, a 14th-century banqueting hall and a medieval royal chapel.

The **Saló del Tinell** is the magnificent 14th-century banqueting hall. Step into this imposing room and you're sure to sense its historical echoes. Beneath the same vast Gothic arches that still span the room, Isabel and Ferdinand received Columbus after his return from the New World. This, too, is where the Holy Inquisition carried out its gruesome trials – legend has it that the walls would move if lies were told here.

Next to the Saló del Tinell, and built into the original Roman city wall, is the **Capella de Santa Àgata** (royal chapel). Its most prized feature is the altarpiece, which depicts scenes from Christ's life in glorious detail. Painted in about 1466 by Catalan artist Jaume Huguet, this ornate altarpiece is considered one of the most important surviving works of Catalan Gothic art. Stairs on the right of the altar lead to a 16th-century bell tower, built upon the original watchtower of the Roman wall. There is a stunning view of Plaça del Rei from the top of the tower.

For most visitors, however, the main attraction of this museum lies underground. Accessed by a lift or walkway, the remains of an entire corner of the Roman town of **Barcino** are incredibly intact. You can see the original city wall and streets, a dye shop and a laundry (which still has faintly visible soap residues). There are factories that produced the Romans' renowned fish sauce and a wine store, complete with intact amphora. A suspended walkway allows you to stroll above a Roman merchant's home, its colourful mosaic floors beautifully displayed. **Adm**

Museu Frederic Marès *eclectic hoard* `6 E3`
Plaça Sant Iu 5–6 • 93 310 5800
» www.museumares.bcn.es Open 10–7 Tue–Sat, 10–3 Sun

The private hoard of sculptor, traveller and magpie-like collector Frederic Marès has produced one of Barcelona's most unusual and eclectic museums. Marès collected everything from sublime Gothic religious imagery and ancient architectural remnants to snuff boxes, cigarette cards and perfume bottles. **Adm**

Catedral de Barcelona *history & art* `6 E3`
Plaça de la Seu • 93 315 1554
» www.catedralbcn.org
Open 8–12:45 & 5:15–7:30 daily

Barcelona's Cathedral is rich in historical and architectural details. The site has been a place of worship from the city's earliest days, and a Roman temple stood here long before the first Christian basilica was built in the 6th century. The present building is medieval, but the façade is a 19th-century Neo-Gothic addition.

Inside, you'll find a glorious symphony of vaulted Gothic arches spanning three large naves. The dominant feature is a beautifully carved choir from the 1390s, but venture into the side chapels too. One of them contains a font where six Taino "Indians" (from what is now the Bahamas) were baptized, having been brought to Spain by Columbus in 1493. Bathed in light filtered through palms and a fountain, the Cathedral's cloister is a spendidly atmospheric retreat, where white geese are kept as symbols of purity.

Shlomo Ben Adret Synagogue `5 D3`
C/Marlet 5 • 93 317 0790
» www.calldebarcelona.org
Open 11–6 Mon–Fri, 11–3 Sat & Sun

Only discovered by chance during the building of a bar, this ancient synagogue is located in the basement of a 13th-century building. It has been painstakingly restored and, 500 years after Spain's expulsion of the Jews, once again contains an Ark and a Menorah. **Adm**

» *The entrance to the Museu Frederic Marès is reached via Plaça Sant Iu, one of Barcelona's prettiest squares*

Museu Tèxtil i d'Indumentària 6 F3

C/Montcada 12 • 93 319 7603

>> www.museutextil.bcn.es Open 10–6 Tue–Sat, 10–3 Sun

Barcelona has always been a fashion-conscious city, and this museum shows what the best-dressed Barcelonins have worn from the Middle Ages to the late 20th century. On the ground floor, the collection focuses on the Gothic to Renaissance periods, continues with Baroque costumes and culminates in the heavily embroidered, full-skirted frocks of the 1800s.

The second floor displays 20th-century attire, and this is where most visitors' eyes light up. Spain's famous couturier, Basque-born Cristóbel Balenciaga, is well represented, as is Paco Rabanne – his 1960s chain-mail mini dress would still be capable of stopping traffic on any street today. The museum's café-restaurant, set in the Gothic courtyard, is one of the most popular and atmospheric in the city. The museum also has an excellent shop, selling clothes and accessories by local designers. **Adm**

Palau de la Virreina *cultural centre* 5 C2

Las Ramblas 99 • 93 301 7775

Open 10–2 & 4–8 Mon–Fri, 10–8 Sat, 11–3 Sun

This 18th-century Neo-Classical palace houses the **Barcelona Institute of Culture**. Its two large exhibition spaces are used to hold an eclectic mix of temporary shows. Highlights of recent years have included a collection of primitive erotic art and an exhibition of posters from the Spanish Civil War.

Contemporary Galleries

A stalwart of the modern scene, **Joan Prats Gallery** (Rambla Catalunya 54; Map 2 E5) has been around since the 1920s. The gallery now shows quirky artists such as Eulàlia Valldosera and Catalan Perejaume. **Maeght Gallery** (C/Montcada 25; Map 6 F3) – the Barcelona counterpart of the prestigious Parisian operation – is based in a beautiful Renaissance palace near the Picasso Museum. **Kowasa Gallery** (C/Mallorca 235; Map 1 D4; www.kowasa.com/gallery) is dedicated to photography, and has a huge collection from masters such as Cartier-Bresson and contemporary photographers like Ouka Lele. On the underground scene, check out art collective **La Santa** (C/Angels 12; Map 5 B1). Most galleries are closed Sunday and Monday.

Museu Picasso *the early years* `6 F3`
C/Montcada 15–23 • 93 319 6310
>> www.museupicasso.bcn.es Open 10–8 Tue–Sun

Picasso arrived in Barcelona in 1895 aged 14, and at once threw himself with gusto into the seedy side of the city, as well as the burgeoning art scene. It was in Paris a few years later that Picasso changed the history of art with paintings such as the groundbreaking *Les Demoiselles d'Avignon* (1907), but Barcelona is where the seeds of that revolution were sown.

Barcelona's Museu Picasso is set in three beautiful interlinked medieval palaces, and its fine collection of more than 3,500 works includes paintings, drawings, prints and ceramics from all of Picasso's artistic periods. It is particularly strong, however, on his formative years. *Man with Beret* (1895) was painted when

Picasso was aged 14, and the allegorical *Science and Charity*, produced two years later, shows the young artist already confident in the techniques of perspective and composition. The museum also has a beautiful collection of works from Picasso's Quatre Gats *(see p30)* period. These are colourful, expressionistic depictions of Barcelonan street life, reflecting the young man's passion for the city.

In 1904, Picasso moved to Paris and embarked upon what has become known as his Blue period. This body of work is well represented, with such masterpieces as the El Greco-inspired *Mad Man* (1904). From Picasso's later years, the museum has an entire room dedicated exclusively to his *Meninas*, a series of 44 meditations on Velázquez's most famous work, *Las Meninas* (1656). **Adm**

Basílica de Santa María del Mar `6 F4`

Plaça de Santa María • 93 310 2390
Open 9–1:30 & 4:30–8 daily (late opening Sun, to 10pm)

Many regard the Basílica de Santa María del Mar as Barcelona's most beautiful building, architecturally superior to the clash of styles of the main Cathedral. This is because the church was built in less than 60 years, between 1329 and 1384, giving the building a unity of style that is almost unique among Gothic churches. The basilica – built in honour of St Mary of the Sea, patron saint of mariners – is considered the pinnacle of Catalan Gothic, a style that favoured slim columns rising to delicate fan vaults.

Architectural connoisseurs who appreciate the purity of the church's form can also thank a group of anti-clerical anarchists who set fire to the building in 1936. They completely destroyed the bulky Baroque altarpiece – a feature of so many Spanish churches – and so returned the basilica to the spacious, uncluttered form that had always been intended.

Museu de la Xocolata *choccy heaven* `6 G3`

Plaça Pons i Clerich • 93 268 7878
>> www.museudelaxocolata.com
Open 10–7 Mon & Wed–Sat, 10–3 Sun

A must for the sweet of tooth, the Museu de Xocolata provides a guide to the origins, history and varieties of the world's favourite comfort food. Extraordinary sculptures demonstrate prodigious chocolate artistry, and the bar serves cups of luscious hot chocolate. **Adm**

CCCB *contemporary culture showcase* `5 B1`

C/Montalegre 5 • 93 306 4100
>> www.cccb.org Open Tue–Sun: check website for times

Located in an early 19th-century paupers' hospital, CCCB stages exhibitions, performances and discussions. It is entered via the building's cloister, and the exhibition spaces are on the upper floors. Its eclectic range of shows has recently included exhibitions on "junk culture" and the Surrealists in Paris. **Adm**

MACBA (Museu d'Art Contemporani de Barcelona)

`5 B1`

Plaça dels Angels 1 • 93 412 0810
>> www.macba.es
Open 11–7:30 Mon & Wed–Fri, 10–8 Sat, 10–3 Sun

Richard Meier's brilliant white building is more than just a home for MACBA; it is a landmark in Barcelona's art scene. Its straight lines and curves create a sinuous flow of light and shadow, and natural light is skilfully used to illuminate the galleries evenly.

The permanent collection has been greatly expanded over the last few years, and focuses mainly on Catalan art from the 1940s to the present day. The first section concentrates on the Dau al Set group – the Catalan Surrealists brought together in the 1940s by Joan Brossa, Barcelona's self-proclaimed "visual poet". His sculpture *Poem-Object* (1956) juxtaposes the head of a broom and domino pieces, echoing Marcel Duchamp's "readymades aided" (such as the famous bicycle wheel on a stool, *Bicycle Wheel*, 1951).

Antoni Tàpies was part of Brossa's Dau al Set group, and the museum has a strong selection from his prolific output. It includes his best "material paintings", which use a variety of different fabrics and substances layered on the canvas. *Ochre Painting* (1959), for example, uses sand, crushed marble and wobbly latex to create a surface of impermanency and movement.

Another important Catalan artist represented at the museum is Miguel Barceló, whose work *Ball de Carn* (Meat Dance, 1994) uses paint, charcoal, paper and latex to reinterpret traditional, studious still life painting through messy Expressionism. The museum has a well-selected group of works by artists of other nationalities, including Jean-Michel Basquiat, Marcel Broodthaers and Joseph Beuys. It also has a strong programme of temporary exhibitions. **Adm**

Art & Architecture

Esglesia de Sant Pau del Camp 5 A4

C/Sant Pau 101 • 93 441 0001
Open 10–2 Mon–Sat

The ancient church of Sant Pau sits incongruously amid the chaotic streets of Barrio Chino, well off the beaten tourist track. It is Barcelona's oldest church and a rare example of Romanesque architecture to survive in the city. As its name (St Paul in the Fields) suggests, when it was founded in the 9th century – and subsequently rebuilt in the 10th and 12th centuries – the church stood in tranquil, rolling pastures outside the city walls.

The building is a wonderful collection of medieval and earlier details, including an entrance with sculpted reliefs of fantastical flora and fauna that dates back to the 10th century. There is also a beautiful 12th-century cloister *(see p144)*.

The founder of the church, Guifré Borrell, is buried here. He was the son of one Wilfred the Hairy, a man often referred to as the "Father of the Catalan Nation".

Museu Marítim *the story of seafaring* 5 B5

Avinguda de les Drassanes • 93 342 9920
>> www.museumaritimbarcelona.org Open 10–8 daily

On entering the Royal Shipyards (in which the museum is housed), you are instantly taken back to the age of galleons and seaborne adventure. The 14th-century stone building, with its huge vaults and soaring arches, is the last complete surviving example of a Gothic shipyard in the world.

The museum's collection offers an enthralling trawl through the history of seafaring, using reconstructions of ancient vessels, as well as antique maps and audio-visual displays, to tell the stories of great voyages of discovery. Dominating the centre of the museum is a reconstruction of John of Austria's *Galera Real*. At 60-m (195-ft) long, this glistening ship is an astonishing replica of the boat that took part in the Battle of Lepanto in 1571. Go up on deck for a close-up view of the elaborately embellished stern which overlooks the 58 oars that would have been manned by slaves. **Adm**

Metrònom *cutting-edge gallery in the heart of the Born* `6 G4`
C/Fusina 9 • 93 268 4298
>> www.metronom-bcn.org Open 11–2 & 5–8 Tue–Sat

The Born area is home not only to trendy clothes shops and bars, but also, since 1980, to one of Barcelona's best alternative art galleries. Metrònom has stayed faithful to its remit of presenting "daring" works of art, which have recently included a collection of erotic underground photography and an exhibition of "living art", consisting of moulds and bacteria that changed and evolved daily.

Pavelló Mies van der Rohe *an icon* `3 A2`
Avinguda del Marqués de Comillas • 93 423 4016
>> www.miesbcn.com Open 10–8 daily

With its effortlessly cool blend of high Modernism and classical serenity, this is arguably the greatest work of Mies van der Rohe. Built as the German pavilion for the 1929 Universal Exhibition and reassembled here in 1986, the steel, glass and marble building is a cornerstone of 20th-century design. **Adm**

CaixaForum *heavyweight exhibitions* `3 A1`
Avinguda Marqués de Comillas 6–8 • 93 476 8600
>> www.fundacio.lacaixa.es Open 10–8 Tue–Sun

The exterior of this former textile factory, designed by Puig i Cadafalch *(see p89)*, incorporates the signature elements of Modernista industrial design: red bricks, blue tiling and Neo-Gothic forms. But Arata Isozaki's renovation of the long-abandoned factory has re-awakened it from within, and transformed it into one of Barcelona's premier cultural centres. His touches of modern functionalism, such as revolving glass doors, escalators and neon lighting, are seamlessly integrated into the structure of the original building.

The large halls of the main exhibition space are dedicated to retrospectives of major artists, such as Dalí, Cartier-Bresson and Rodin, while the smaller space is used to hold shows by contemporary artists. The CaixaForum is also a venue for two of Barcelona's best music festivals: Festival de Música Antiga *(see p16)* and autumn's World Music Festival.

>> There are English-speaking guided visits to the Pavelló Mies van der Rohe from 5 to 7pm Wednesday & Friday

Art & Architecture

MNAC (Museu Nacional d'Art de Catalunya) 3 A2

1,000 years of Catalan art
Parc de Montjuïc, Palau Nacional • 93 622 0360
>> www.mnac.es Open 10–7 Tue–Sat, 10–2:30 Sun

The dream of a national museum of Catalan art has finally materialized after decades of practical and political impediments. Thankfully, the result has left no one disappointed. MNAC brings together much of the region's greatest art to create a cultural narrative that spans more than 1,000 years. And all of this is contained within the spectacular Palau Nacional.

The last stage of the enormous project to convert the giant Neo-Classical edifice (built for the Universal Exhibition of 1929) into Barcelona's premier museum was completed at the beginning of 2005. Italian architect Gae Aulenti has transformed the grand and somewhat intimidating space into a succession of smaller and more intimate gallery spaces. The collection follows a chronological path, beginning on the ground floor with extraordinary Romanesque frescoes, brought here from isolated churches in the Catalan Pyrenées. Particularly striking is the vivid *Christ in Majesty* from the fresco (circa 1123) of the Sant Climent church in Taüll. The museum also has a rich collection of Catalan Gothic art, including a mural of around 1285 that depicts, in a visual narrative, the conquest of Mallorca by the Catalan knights.

The Thyssen-Bornemisza collection (recently moved here from the Monestir de Pedralbes, *see p90*) offers a good opportunity to enjoy masterpieces by Canaletto, Velázquez and Goya, and Fra Angelico's exquisite *Virgen de la Humildad* (1435). The recently opened upper floors show key works from the golden age of Catalan Modernisme and 20th-century art by the likes of Dalí and Tàpies. Also on the top floor is a beautiful collection of furniture by Gaudí's collaborator Gaspar Homar. MNAC's collection is extraordinarily rich, and only the bravest will attempt it all in one visit. **Adm**

Fundació Joan Miró _modern art shrine_ `3 B3`
Parc de Montjuïc • 93 443 9470
» www.bcn.fjmiro.es Open 10–8 Tue–Sat (Oct–Jun: to 7),
10–2:30 Sun (late opening Thu, to 9:30)

Josep Lluís Sert's sleek assortment of geometric shapes has become a classic and often-copied form in the realm of museum architecture. It provides the perfect setting for the stunningly visual art of Joan Miró. The artist was, of course, one of the pioneers of Modernism – along with avant-garde painters such as Picasso, Gris and Dalí, he shook up the Paris art world of the early 20th century. Towards the end of his long and prolific career, he chose to establish this foundation in his home town. Miró charged his long-time friend, Catalan architect Sert, with the realization of the project, which was completed in 1975.

Sert, a disciple of arch-Modernist Le Corbusier, mixed the rationalist modern approach with more traditional Mediterranean concepts of light and space.

The galleries are lit mostly by natural light, which comes in indirectly through lantern windows. The cool deflected light sets off the warm colours of Miró's art.

The foundation's collection takes in seven decades of the artist's work, starting with his experiments as a teenager (the Impressionist-inspired landscape _Hermitage at Sant Joan de Horta_, 1913) and his move towards abstraction, such as _The Bottle_ (1924). There are also early flirtations with Surrealism (_Man and Woman in Front of a Pile of Excrement_, 1935). Most of the work from this period onwards, including a number of sculptures and a huge tapestry, concentrates on the stylistic language that became the artist's trademark: strong primary colours and simple organic forms.

An additional highlight of the museum is a work by Miró's friend Alexander Calder. Calder's kinetic sculpture _Mercury Fountain_ (1937) – a hypnotic play of constant, liquid movement using mercury and iron – was created as an anti-fascist tribute. **Adm**

» _Dotted with some of Miró's wonderful sculptures, the Fundació's terrace café is a great spot for lunch_

Art & Architecture

Museu Egipci de Barcelona `2 E4`

C/Valencia 284 • 93 488 0188
combined ticket with Fundación Francisco Godia
>> www.fundclos.com Open 10–8 Mon–Sat, 10–2 Sun

Barcelona's Egyptian museum presents a fascinating
selection of artifacts (including mummified cats and
falcons) culled from 3,000 years of Egyptian history.
It also hosts temporary exhibitions on subjects such
as the role of women in ancient Egypt. **Adm**

Fundación Francisco Godia `2 E4`

C/Valencia 284 pral • 93 272 3180 • combined ticket with
Museu Egipci de Barcelona
>> www.fundacionfgodia.org Open 10–8 Wed–Mon

The collection of playboy Formula 1 driver and art con-
noisseur Francisco Godia (1921–90) is best known
for its Spanish Gothic and Romanesque medieval art.
However, the museum also displays works by Catalan
painters such as Casas, Tàpies and Miró. **Adm**

Fundació Antoni Tàpies *art for the arty* `2 E4`

C/Aragó 255 • 93 487 0315
>> www.fundaciotapies.org Open 10–8 Tue–Sun

The foundation of Barcelona's most internationally
celebrated living artist (1923–) is sited in a former
publishing house, built by the Modernista architect
Domènech i Montaner. The orderliness of this rather
restrained bit of 19th-century architecture provides an
interesting contrast with Tàpies' often wild artistic
adventures involving a whole host of media.
Sculpture, painting and printing, as well as far more
unorthodox assemblages, are all part of the artist's
Abstract Expressionist oeuvre. A good selection of his
work can be seen on the top floor, but it is above this
that you'll find his most eye-catching piece. *Cloud and
Chair* occupies the entire roof of the building with a
spaghetti-like mass of wires and tubes.

   The ground floor is given over to temporary shows
by international contemporary artists, such as
Damien Hirst and Steve McQueen. **Adm**

For the very latest on Barcelona go to >> **www.realcity.dk.com**

Modernista Masterworks *architectural gems*

In the late 19th century, Art Nouveau swept Europe, with its stylized natural forms, bright colours and sinuous lines. In Barcelona, the arrival of this style coincided with the emergence of an extraordinarily talented group of artists, a growing feeling of national confidence and an economic boom. The result of such fortune was Modernisme, an artistic movement that found its greatest expression in architecture.

Between 1900 and 1907, in an epic battle for creative supremacy, three of Modernisme's greatest exponents squared off with designs for buildings that are grouped on Passeig de Gràcia. Together, they are known as the "Mansana de la Discòrdia" (Block of Discord; Map 2 E5), due to their wildly conflicting styles.

Domènech i Montaner created the **Casa Lleó Morera** (closed to the public), an exuberant, highly decorative building with a fairy-tale minaret. Puig i Cadafalch contributed the **Casa Amatller** (open at ground-floor

level only), a medievalist fantasy of turrets, shiny ceramics and a "gallery of grotesques" (a frieze of gargoyles). Next door stands one of Gaudí's greatest works, the magical **Casa Batlló** *(see p76)*.

At the beginning of the 20th century, Barcelona considered Domènech i Montaner its greatest architect, and he was commissioned to create two of the city's most important buildings (both now have UNESCO World Heritage status). **Hospital de Sant Pau** (C/Sant Antoni María Claret; Map 2 H3; 90 2076 621 for visitor info) was Modernisme's greatest civic work, a "garden city" of 17 pavilions, each with its own collection of expressive sculptures, murals and mosaics. Montaner then created the **Palau de la Música Catalana** *(see p98)*, perhaps the world's most flamboyant concert hall. The interior is an explosion of decoration, with stained glass and mosaic-encrusted sculptures of muses, musicians and charging Valkyries. The overall effect is spellbinding.

Palau Reial de Pedralbes *stately home*
Avinguda Diagonal 686 • 93 280 5024 • Palau Reial metro
Open 10–6 Tue–Sat, 10–3 Sun (free first Sun of the month)

With its tranquil gardens, ample courtyard, marble staircase and graceful entrance hall, the Palau Reial seems far removed from the hustle and bustle of the city outside its doors. It is now home to two museums. The **Museu de Ceràmica** (www.museuceramica.bcn. es) has an excellent selection of ceramics, from Moorish storage vessels and tiles to works by the Modernistas and Picasso and Miró. The **Museu de les Arts Decoratives** (www.museuartsdecoratives. bcn.es) provides a whirlwind review of the decorative arts in Barcelona, from the 12th century to the 21st, and has a lively programme of design exhibitions.

Just a few minutes' walk from the Palau Reial is the **Monestir de Pedralbes** (Baixada del Monestir 9), a 14th-century convent that, until recently, housed the Thyssen-Bornemisza collection. Visit it (10–2 Tue–Sun) for the beautiful three-storey cloister. **Adm for each**

Teatre-Museu Dalí *Sur-reality show*
Plaça Gala-Salvador Dalí 5, Figueres • 97 267 7500 • RENFE train from BCN Sants or Passeig de Gràcia to Figueres (2hrs)
≫ www.salvador-dali.org Open Jul–Sep: 9–7:45 daily; Oct–Jun: 10:30–5:45 Wed–Mon

Salvador Dalí – Surrealist jester and self-proclaimed artistic genius – transformed his home town's theatre into a museum in 1974. The building was reborn with countless Dalíesque touches, including giant eggs atop the roof and sculpted loaves of bread studding the walls. It has since become one of Spain's most visited museums, with crowds queuing to experience what could be described as a Surrealist theme park.

Highlights include Dalí's 3-D portrait of Mae West – which features his famous "pair of lips" sofa – and a huge ceiling fresco in the Wind Palace Room. The fresco depicts the artist and his partner Gala standing astride the roof of heaven like demigods. A place of eccentricity, humour and astonishing art, the museum is also the burial place of Dalí, who died in 1984. **Adm**

Old Girona *architectural gem of the Middle Ages*

RENFE train from BCN Sants or Passeig de Gràcia (1hr 20min)
➤➤ www.lacatedraldegirona.com

In Girona, a city full of sublime medieval architecture, the **cathedral** (Adm) is the jewel in the crown. It is reached by a stairway of 90 steps, which creates a suitably dramatic approach to the looming Baroque façade of the building. The entrance gives way to a largely Gothic interior, which includes the widest nave of this kind in the world. The 14th-century silver altarpiece by Bartomeu i Andreu incorporates elements from a 12th-century Romanesque altar. This priceless object was saved during the Civil War by being shipped to Paris. Now it can be appreciated in all its glory; 10 of the 12 statues that once presided over the Apostle's Gate were, alas, not so fortunate.

The atmospheric cloister and most of the bell tower are all that remain of the original Romanesque church. Reliefs that decorate the cloister's columns portray the torments of hell in lurid detail, and were designed to impress upon young novices the need for stricture.

The cathedral's **museum** holds a fabulous *Tapestry of the Creation* – a unique 12th-century wall-hanging that depicts Christ creating the world. Bizarre half-fish, half-bird creatures appear, having clearly arisen from the artist's overly fertile imagination.

The historic centre of Girona is one of the best-preserved medieval cities in Europe, giving visitors the opportunity to walk through streets that have changed little in 500 years. One of the city's earliest extant buildings is the **Banys Àrabs** (Arab Baths; Adm) on C/Ferran el Catòlic. The name is a little misleading, however. The baths were built in the late 12th century in the Mudéjar-Romanesque style (which incorporated elements of Arab architecture), but were probably first used by the city's Jewish population, which was considerable in the Middle Ages. Much later, in the 17th century, the baths were subsumed into a Capuchin convent, and used as a kitchen and laundry.

Built on the Onyar, Girona is also famous for the Venetian-style houses that line the river. View these multicoloured buildings from the **Pont de Pedra**.

➤➤ *For a fantastic place to eat in Girona,* see Celler de Can Roca, p46

performance

For a relatively small city, Barcelona has a gargantuan personality and some of the most magnificent performance spaces in the world. From internationally recognized concert halls, such as the Palau de la Música Catalana and the Liceu Opera House, to fringe theatres, drag cabarets and a world-class live music scene, this city has it all. Handily, most venues are concentrated in the compact city centre.

PERFORMANCE

Barcelona goes from strength to strength in the world of performing arts, and now attracts an impressive range of artists and musicians. In recent years festivals like the Grec *(see p17)*, which mixes world-class theatre with avant-garde dance and music, and the International Jazz Festival *(see p18)* have made the city an important destination for roving festival-goers. But at any time of the year I love the city's intimate venues: places like Harlem Jazz Club, one-off cinemas such as Méliès and cabaret venue Luz de Gas.

Tara Stevens

Classical Glamour

Catalunya has a strong musical tradition. It boasts superb orchestras and choirs, and has some extraordinary venues for classical music. The **Liceu** *(see p96)* is one of the most technically advanced concert halls in Europe, while at the **Palau de la Música Catalana** *(see p98)* music comes to life theatrically beneath a stained-glass cupola.

Dancing in the City

Large venues such as **Teatre Poliorama** *(see p97)* and **Mercat de les Flors** *(see p100)* are good for ballets (especially at Christmas) and large-scale flamenco extravaganzas. However, a more intense atmosphere is found at smaller venues, such as **Tinta Roja** *(see p101)*, for genuine Argentinian tango, and **Teatre Lliure** *(see p99)* for modern dance.

Treading the Boards

Demand for good theatre is growing in Barcelona. Venues such as the **Teatre Lliure** *(see p99)* and the **Mercat de les Flors** *(see p100)* show cutting-edge productions from New York and London, while the **Teatre Nacional de Catalunya** *(see p102)* is gradually finding its feet with a feast of quality Catalan, Spanish and English-language productions.

choice acts

Live Bands

The world's biggest bands are no different to anyone else: they all love an excuse to come to Barcelona, and Barcelona loves to receive them. The city is now one of Europe's number one spots for rock festivals, the best of which is **Sónar** *(see p16)*. At any time of year, check out **Razzmatazz** *(see p104)* and smouldering jazz club **Harlem** *(see p97)*.

Cabaret

El Cangrejo *(see p99)* was home to the city's first drag show, and the venue continues with a bawdy spirit; dirty jokes and sequinned ball gowns are all part of a thoroughly outrageous night out. **Luz de Gas** *(see p103)* offers a more upmarket, though still essentially kitsch, take on cabaret, with frilly table lamps and a 19th-century ambience.

Stars of the Silver Screen

Catalans take film seriously, and Barcelona has some excellent V.O. (original version) cinemas. Check out the **Méliès** *(see p102)* for art house and Hollywood classics, and **Renoir Floridablanca** *(see p103)* and the **FilmoTeca de la Generalitat de Catalunya** *(see p102)* for strong programmes of European and independent cinema.

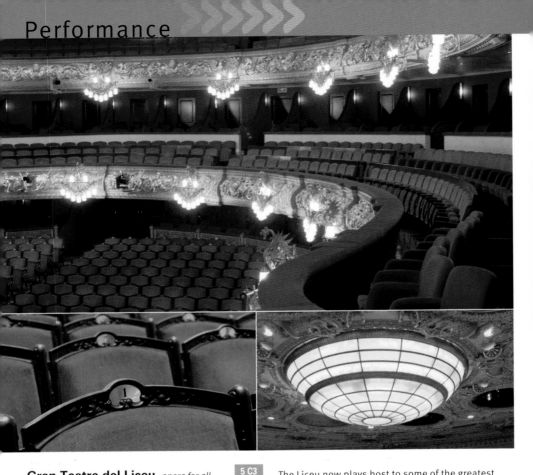

Gran Teatre del Liceu *opera for all* `5 C3`
Las Ramblas 51–9 • 93 485 9914
»» www.liceubarcelona.com Box office 2–8:30 Mon–Fri;
Open to visitors 10–2 daily; guided tours at 10

One of Europe's finest opera houses, the Liceu is also one of the world's most sophisticated, thanks to a fire in 1994. Normally a conflagration wouldn't be good news for a theatre, but in this case it forced the management to undertake a long-overdue modernization. The result is a copy of the 1847 building, constructed at three times its original size and equipped with state-of-the-art stage technology.

The Liceu now plays host to some of the greatest voices in the world of opera, including Placido Domingo, Natalie Dessay and Juan Diego Florez.

The theatre presents as many as 11 different productions in any given season, as well as additional performances of ballet, chamber music, occasional cinema screenings and special children's operas. Ticket prices range from as little as €7.50 to more than €150. You can also get discounted seats for second cast performances. This policy is aimed at making a night at the opera more accessible to the masses – something that Barcelona is always keen to promote.

Teatre Poliorama *popular theatre* `5 C2`
Las Ramblas 115 • 93 317 7599
>> www.teatrepoliorama.com Box office 5–8 Tue–Sat

A hugely popular venue, Teatre Poliorama trades on crowd-pleasing musical adaptations, such as *Le Petit Dalí* (Little Dalí) and *Robin, Príncep de Lladres* (Robin, Prince of Thieves). Such performances can easily be enjoyed without speaking the language and are cheap, too. Dance and comedy productions also feature.

Harlem Jazz Club *live jazz* `5 D4`
C/Comtessa de Sobradiel 8 • 93 310 0755
Entry charged Fri–Sun only (pay at the door)

The vibe remains sizzling and sexy at one of the city's pioneering venues for jazz. Attracting legions of loyal fans every night of the week, Harlem is everything a jazz club should be – small, smoky and committed to the music. Expect everything from soulful, bluesy saxophone musings to high-tempo Latin rhythms.

Music in Parc de la Ciutadella `7 A3`
L'Hivernacle de la Ciutadella *(see p115)*
Swing on Sundays (from noon in winter; 6–8pm in summer)
>> www.bcnswing.org

Barcelona's central park is cherished as one of the few truly green spaces in the city. It is a hive of music and dance events, and on Sundays throughout the year local dancers jive and jitterbug to swing in the bandstand. The spectacular 19th-century wrought-iron and glass conservatory, L'Hivernacle, is the heart of the park, and provides the focus for jazz and opera performances in summer – check in the *Guía del Ocio (see p22)* for details.

L'Hivernacle is also the spot for occasional evening performances of jazz and blues, most notably in October, when it has its own mini-festival. The *fin-de-siècle* ambience makes it one of the most atmospheric venues in the city. On a balmy evening, few experiences can compare with being serenaded by a jazz quartet while sipping a glass of chilled white wine.

>> *For more on Parc de la Ciutadella,* see p143

Palau de la Música Catalana `6 F1`

C/Sant Francesc de Paula 2 • 90 244 2882

>> www.palaumusica.org Box office: 10–9 Mon–Sat, 1hr before concerts Sun (1 week advance booking recommended)

Originally built to house the Catalan Choral Society, Lluís Domènech I Montaner's Modernista marvel *(see also p89)* was finished in 1908. Its early years were crucial to the auditorium's success, and its position as a heavyweight on the international arts scene was secured by a remarkable series of concerts. Among them was a performance by the Berlin Philharmonic Orchestra, conducted by the great early-20th century German composer Richard Strauss.

Recently, the venue has added to its repertoire a series of Sunday afternoon and themed concerts at substantially discounted prices, as well as an extensive programme of classical music for children. It is worth getting tickets to see any performance in the richly decorated concert hall, with its mesmerizing glass-domed ceiling. Failing that, take a guided tour – they are conducted daily (10am–3:30pm) in Catalan, Spanish and English, and cost €8.

El Cangrejo *drag cabaret*

5 B5

C/Montserrat 9 • 93 301 2978
Open Tue–Sun from 9pm

One of Barcelona's most emblematic night spots, El Cangrejo was the city's original drag cabaret, attracting a mixed bag of characters from the streets of the Barrio Chino in the lower Raval. This area earned itself a reputation as the city's most depraved neighbourhood in the 19th and early 20th centuries, and El Cangrejo fits right in with that atmosphere of libertine bohemia – a place of "cheap love and rough brandy", as Spanish writer Camilo José Cela described it.

Housed in a dungeon-like bar in the dark recesses of the barrio, El Cangrejo's flavour is part Jean Genet, part Pedro Almodóvar. Barcelona's celebrity drag queen Carmen de Mairena performs on Friday and Saturday nights, along with an entourage of glamorous lady-boys. Expect outrageous costumes, empassioned *boleros* (Spanish love songs), Gloria Gaynor mime-alongs and plenty of cheeky repartee.

Palau Sant Jordi *rock on a grand scale*

3 A3

Passeig Olímpic 5–7 • 93 426 2089
» www.agendabcn.com

Designed by the Japanese architect Arata Isozaki, the futuristic Palau Sant Jordi looks like a cool white flying saucer. With a capacity for 20,000 within, it is the venue of choice for big-name acts such as Bruce Springsteen, U2 and Phil Collins, with the occasional heavy metal band thrown in to test the sound system.

Teatre Lliure *radical drama, modern dance*

3 B2

Plaça de Margarida Xirgú 1 • 93 289 2770
» www.teatrelliure.com

Barcelona's Teatre Lliure is fast gaining a reputation as the best in town thanks to the vision of director Àlex Rigola. The programming includes some English-language productions and contemporary dance, alongside Catalan and Spanish theatre. Performances on Wednesday nights are presented with English subtitles.

Performance

Teatre Grec *starlit open-air theatre* `3 B3`
Passeig de Santa Madrona 36, Parc de Montjuïc
>> www.bcn.es/grec Information & tickets from the Institut de Cultura, Palau de la Virreina *(see p80)*

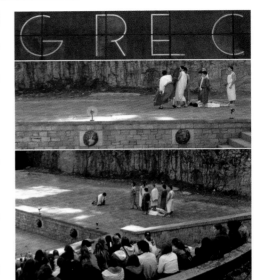

Barcelona's only open-air theatre springs to life each summer, between June and August. This is when the annual **Festival del Grec** takes place, presenting classical and world music, as well as drama and dance. The festival's venues are scattered right across the city, but nowhere beats this theatre when it comes to moonlit magic – if you have the chance to see anything here, take it. Built in the late 19th century in imitation of a Greek amphitheatre, Teatre Grec is set amid a verdant wood on the slopes of Montjuïc. It is an absolutely enchanting spot to see a ballet or listen to a classical concert.

The festival is currently one of the most important summertime events on the Barcelona calendar, attracting a host of theatre productions, international musicians and dance companies *(see also p17)*.

El Tablao de Carmen *intro to flamenco* `3 A1`
Poble Espanyol • 93 325 6895
>> www.tablaodecarmen.com Open from 7pm Tue–Sun

This "movie-set" taverna pays homage to Carmen Amaya – a famous flamenco dancer from the old Somorrostro district of Barcelona (now Vila Olímpica). It was on this site that she made her debut in front of King Alfonso XIII in 1929. Though clearly touristy, this is a good place to see your first flamenco.

Mercat de les Flors *experimental drama* `3 B2`
C/Lleida 59 • 93 426 1875
>> www.mercatflors.org
Box office open 1hr before performances begin

Renowned for experimental work, Mercat de les Flors has become one of the most respected theatres in Barcelona. Here, live performances are frequently mixed with contemporary media, such as video and the Internet. Art exhibitions are also hosted.

Tinta Roja *true tango*

3 C2

C/Creu dels Molers 17 • 93 443 3243
>> www.tintaroja.net Open from 8pm Wed–Sun; closed mid- to late Aug; tickets available 1hr before performances

There is but one proper tango bar in the city and this is it: a former textile factory that has been converted into a venue that smoulders with sexiness. It is run by two dancers who used to perform in Argentina, and they give the place its authenticity, as do the faded posters and collected artifacts of their days in the South American limelight.

Beyond a small, intimate bar, a corridor opens onto a Moulin-Rouge-style theatre, complete with swinging trapeze, red velvet curtains, gilded picture frames and the kind of deep, comfy sofas you could disappear in. There are performances of some sort – tango usually, though not exclusively – most Thursday, Friday and Saturday nights. The theatre also plays host to fringe companies staging wacky productions, as well as a varied array of dance and musical spectacles.

RCD Espanyol *Barcelona's other team*

3 A3

Estadi Olímpic de Montjuïc • 93 423 8644
>> www.rcdespanyol.com Ticket office 9:30–1:30, 5–8 Mon–Fri

Barcelona's second-most-successful football team play their home matches in the Neo-Classical Estadi Olímpic, which was built for the 1992 Olympics. It's a beautiful setting for a game, though Espanyol rarely more than half-fill the stadium. Therefore, tickets are easy to obtain, but the atmosphere is a little sleepy.

Buying Tickets

All of the big venues have their own box offices, and it's worth checking their respective websites for discounted tickets for second cast, Sunday afternoon or other special performances. You can also get tickets in advance from **Servicaixa de La Caixa** (www.servicaixa.com); **Tel-Entrada de Caixa Catalunya** (www.telentrada.com); and **El Corte**
Inglés (www.elcorteingles.com). Savings of up to 50% can be made by buying theatre tickets through **Tiquet-3** at the Tourist Office on Plaça Catalunya.

Football tickets can be purchased from the ticket offices at the **Camp Nou** *(see p105)* or **Estadi Olímpic** in advance, or by turning up an hour beforehand for less important games. **www.barcelona-football-tickets.com** is reliable, but more expensive.

Performance

Teatre Nacional de Catalunya `7 B1`
Plaça de les Arts 1 • 93 306 5700
» www.tnc.es Box office 3–9 Tue–Sat, 3–6 Sun

Designed by Ricard Bofill, the seat of Catalan theatre
is an impressive venue – a bold structure of glass
walls, thrusting columns and a metallic roof. The
productions thus far have yet to stir the passions of
regular theatre-goers, but it is surely only a matter of
time before the TNC strikes a chord with its audience.

Méliès *cinema for cineastes* `1 C5`
C/Villarroel 102 • 93 451 0051
Box office 3:30–11 daily, depending on screening times

Named after one of the pioneers of European film,
this is very much a film-lover's cinema. Its monthly-
changing programme of Hollywood classics, golden
oldies, film noir and art house movies is usually
themed around a genre or director, such as Alfred
Hitchcock or Fellini. Double-bills are a bargain.

FilmoTeca de la Generalitat de Catalunya *film for the cultured masses* `1 B3`
Avinguda Sarria 31–3 • 93 410 7590
Tickets available 1hr before each screening; closed Aug

Its home may be a rather nondescript building in the
upper reaches of the Eixample (there are plans to
move to a Raval location in 2007), but what makes
the FilmoTeca so special is not its auditorium but its
screenings. They are second to none, and offer an
eclectic mix of cinematic styles and themes.

The programme is unusual in the way that it pairs a
"film of the month" with films in fortnightly-changing
themed series. This means that features may be linked
by relatively obscure connections, such as their musical scores sharing the same composer. An odd arrangement, it is nevertheless one that works, and such
quirks make the cinema all the more loveable. In February, the best films of the previous year are shown,
and each spring the FilmoTeca screens the films of all
the Goya nominees (Spain's equivalent of the Oscars).

Coliseum *grand film house* `4 F1`

Gran Via de les Corts Catalanes 595 • 93 317 1448
» www.grupbalana.com Box office approx 30mins prior to film

One of the oldest cinemas in Barcelona, the Coliseum is styled upon Paris's famous opera house. Its whimsical flourishes and ornate decor transform a night at the movies into a thoroughly grand affair. Unfortunately for non-Spanish speakers, all the movies shown are either voiced in, or dubbed into, Spanish.

Renoir Floridablanca *screens galore* `3 D1`

C/Floridablanca 135 • 902 888 902
» www.cinesrenoir.com Box office approx 30mins prior to film

The Renoir Group stands out for screening high-quality films in small, intimate theatres. Floridablanca is a relatively new seven-screen addition to the chain, showing movies that are more off-beat than the usual Hollywood fare. This is borne out by a strong programme of European films (with Spanish subtitles).

Rooftop Jazz at La Pedrera `2 E4`

Passeig de Gràcia 92–C • 90 2400 973
Open 15 Jun–30 Jul: 9pm–1am Fri & Sat

Gaudí's undulating rooftop is the most dramatic part of his famous apartment block, otherwise known as Casa Milà *(see p76)*. In the summer months it is among the classiest venues to catch one of the jazz quartets who perform regularly, as the smart clientele sips cava while admiring the skyline.

Luz de Gas *cabaret revisited* `1 C2`

C/Muntaner 246 • 93 209 7711
» www.luzdegas.com
Box office opens about 1hr before the start of performances

This kitsch modern cabaret is reminiscent of the music halls of the 19th century, and plays host to musicians from a wide variety of genres, from Dixieland to show classics. Sit back, relax over a cocktail and re-live a golden past.

L'Auditori de Barcelona *fine acoustics* `7 B1`

C/Lepant 150 • 90 210 1212
» www.auditori.org
Box office noon–9pm Mon–Sat, 1hr before concerts Sun

Home to the prize-winning Barcelona Symphony Orchestra, L'Auditori sits next to Catalunya's national theatre, the TNC. The sleek building boasts state-of-the-art technology, making it one of the finest venues in Spain for orchestral performances.

» *Aficionados of the silver screen can buy blocks of 10 or 50 tickets for the FilmoTeca at massive discounts*

Razzmatazz *live music and DJ sets* 7 B2
C/Pamplona 88 • 93 320 8200
» www.salarazzmatazz.com Tickets available from
www.ticktackticket.com or on door, depending on event

With five distinct spaces – each more groovy than the last – "Razz" has become as much a destination for travelling music fans as the Sagrada Família is for culture junkies. The musical spectrum for live acts ranges from the edgy sophistication of Elvis Costello to the unabashed drum-thumping of Megadeth.

If a jam-packed repertoire of live music doesn't take your fancy, the club rooms probably will. Razz Club attracts a who's who of DJs, including The Chemical Brothers, The Glimmer Twins and Howie B. The techno and electronica in the Loft Club thuds and whirs for hard core aficionados, while the vibe in Lolita is more chilled and intimate. The Pop Bar is a sugar-coated playroom for the fashion set, while the Temple Beat Room adds yet more variety to what most agree is an unstoppable party machine. Enjoy.

Bikini *worthy stalwart of the club scene* 1 B2
C/Déu i Mata 105 • 93 322 0800
» www.bikinibcn.com Ticket purchasing varies; check website

One of Barcelona's oldest discos and live venues, Bikini opened in 1953 and immediately became a benchmark for all that was hip and groovy. Amazingly for a city in which the tides of fashion flow fast, Bikini has stood the test of time. Chill in the Dry Room or head to the Arutanga Room for steamy, sultry salsa.

The Sporting Life
When they're not plugged into mini-transistors listening to the latest football scores, chances are Barcelonins will be tuned into the **basketball** during the season (Sep–May). This is the city's second sporting love. Confusingly, Barcelona's top team is, like its main football team, called **FC Barcelona**. You can get tickets for thrilling league and European games at the **Palau Blaugrana** (Avinguda Arístides Maillol; www.fcbarcelona.com) the day before an event. The multi-functional Palau Blaugrana also hosts **roller hockey** games (Oct–May).

Barcelona is an increasingly popular **surfing** destination in the winter months, with several competitions taking place between November and April on local beaches (check www.acsurf.org for details).

FC Barcelona *theatre of passion*

Camp Nou, Avinguda Arístides Maillol • 93 496 3600
» www.fcbarcelona.com • Collblanc metro
Ticket office 9–1:30 & 3:30–6 Mon–Thu, 9–2:30 Fri

Built in 1957, the cauldron-like Camp Nou is the largest football stadium in Europe, with a capacity of 98,000. "Barça" are, in the words of the club motto "more than just a club", being for many a sporting representation of Catalan nationalism. Barcelona traditionally reserve their greatest rivalry for Real Madrid – more often than not they are the two teams vying for top spot in La Liga (Spain's premier league). When Barça are doing well, the stadium fills and generates a terrific atmosphere; a poor performance can be greeted with the *pañolada* – a mass waving of white handkerchiefs and a cacophony of boos. Tickets can be hard to get, though a limited number do go on sale at the stadium in match week. It's worth the effort to obtain one, as a stirring Barcelona victory in this famous stadium is an unforgettable experience.

» *For advice on buying tickets for football matches, as well as other performance events,* see p101

bars & clubs

Style rules supreme in design-obsessed Barcelona. Slink around with the fashion pack in chrome-filled cocktail bars and beachfront lounge clubs, check out the underground vibe in the old city's hidden haunts, or chill in a boho-chic café. And when you've had your fill of super-slick design, hang out with the old-timers in traditional tapas bars that offer wine from the barrel and tasty snacks.

BARS & CLUBS

For all its stylishness, the nightlife scene in Barcelona is surprisingly laid-back. The lack of queues, velvet ropes and fashion police is refreshing and can make other cities look neurotic by comparison. The most glamorous celebrity haunts are found in the Eixample, but I prefer the whiff of bohemian romance in the absinthe-scented bars of the Old City. The nightlife is great year round, but to my mind it is at its best in summer, when the party moves outdoors to the beaches and rooftops.

Mary-Ann Gallagher

Design Bars

Three of the best for sublime design are **Fonfone** *(see p111)*, where retro cool meets space-age chic; **Oven** *(see p127)*, a DJ-owned lounge bar-restaurant in a converted warehouse, with outsized art and scarlet sofas; and funky **Pilé 43** *(see p112)*, where all the furniture is for sale, from the plastic-fantastic ashtrays to the 1950s-style bar stools.

Traditional Bars

At Barcelona's oldest bar, the **Marsella** *(see p118)*, lazy paddle fans flap over marble-topped tables and huge mirrors, while at **Bar Pastís** *(see p116)*, another throwback to a vanished world, cabaret is performed on a miniature stage. Cosy and wood-panelled, the **Pipa Club** *(see p112)* is the perfect antidote to Barcelona's cool style scene.

Outdoor Bars and Clubs

It's impossible to resist the glamorous allure of club **Elephant** *(see p126)*, a Modernista mansion where curtained beds, lamps and candles are scattered throughout the gardens. **Danzatoria** *(see p127)* also throws open its gorgeous gardens in summer. Down at the beach, **CDLC** *(see p123)* and **Sal** *(see p124)* have breezy, seafront terraces.

choice nightlife

Wine and Cava Bars

Sophisticated **Ginger** *(see p111)* offers a wide range of wines and cavas, including an unusual fruity red cava – perfect at the end of a hot day. Little neighbourhood bar **La Bodegueta del Xampú** *(see p125)* is particularly good for the Catalan fizz, and at **La Palma** *(see p112)* hearty local wine is served up in earthenware jugs.

Gay Bars and Clubs

The two classic clubs on Barcelona's gay scene are **Metro** *(see p119)* and **Salvation** *(see p122)*, both with dark rooms and plenty of action. For a buffed, toned and seriously beautiful crowd, head for **Space** *(see p124)*, one of scores of regular gay party nights. And don't forget that the gay mecca of **Sitges** *(see p138)* is just a short train-ride away.

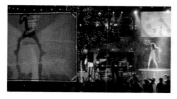

Dance Clubs

Dot *(see p111)* may be the smallest club in town, but it's still one of the hottest, and the line-up of top international and local DJs can't be beaten. **La Paloma** *(see p118)* is the gorgeous setting for the excellent Thursday-night Bongo Lounge, while dedicated fans of electronic music should head to **Zentraus** *(see p119)* in the heart of the Raval.

Bars & Clubs

Bar La Plata *cheerful old-timer*
5 D5

C/Mercè 28 • 93 315 1009
Open 9am–4pm & 6–11pm daily

A survivor from the days when Barcelona was a scruffy port, this tiny, tile-lined *tasca* serves up rough but tasty local wine directly from wooden barrels behind the bar. Such wine is the perfect accompaniment to a plate of succulent grilled sardines or whitebait. Old-timers line the bar, bemused by the passing tourists.

Boadas *Art Deco cocktail bar*
5 C1

C/Tallers 1 • 93 318 8826
>> www.bongust.com/boadas Open noon–2 or 3am Mon–Sat

Having learned his trade at the famed Floridita Bar in Havana, Miquel Boadas opened this Art Deco gem in 1933. Little has changed since, and the impeccable waiters and gleaming chrome recall a more glamorous era. Drinkers from Hemingway to Dalí have propped up the bar, and Miró obliged with a sketch or two.

Bosc de les Fades *fairytale decor*
5 C5

Passatje de la Banca • 93 317 2649
Open 10:30am–2am Mon–Wed, 10:30am–3am Thu–Sun

Welcome to fairyland: pull up a chair in an enchanted, lantern-lit forest, with hooting owls and a whispering breeze, or linger in the salon, with its trompe l'oeil decoration, statuettes and flickering candlelight. By day, this is the Wax Museum café, while at night it becomes a romantic spot for an intimate tête-à-tête.

Café Royale *slick lounge-bar*
5 C4

C/Nou de Zurbano 3 • 93 412 1433
Open 6pm–2:30am Sun–Thu, 6pm–3am Fri & Sat

Spanish film director Pedro Almodóvar threw his celebration bash at this funky lounge-bar after winning the Goya prize for *Todo Sobre Mi Madre* (*All About My Mother*, 1999). Perhaps he was flattered by the kitschy decor that's inspired by his films. You'll have to arrive early to bag one of the designer sofas.

Dot *hip moves and grooves* `5 C4`
C/Nou de Sant Francesc 7 • 93 302 7026
>> www.dotlightclub.com Open 10pm–3am Tue–Sun

One of the smallest clubs in the city, Dot has a big reputation. Head through the space-age doorway into the tiny, red-lit bar to hear the hottest international DJs playing the latest house, funk, breaks and hip-hop. A loungey crowd laps it up, mesmerized by projections and vintage films flickering on the walls.

Fonfone *funky neon-lit bar* `5 C4`
C/Escudellers 24 • 93 317 1424
>> www.fonfone.com
Open 10pm–2:30am Mon–Thu, 10pm–3am Fri & Sat

Retro kitsch meets futuristic neon in Fonfone, with its geometric tiles, green lights in the shape of circuit boards, and red and orange lights made of Lego. Local hipsters love the bar's electro-dance music and relaxed chill-out area with floaty audio-visuals.

Ginger *retro cocktail bar* `6 E4`
C/Palma de Sant Just 1 • 93 310 5309
Open 7pm–2:30am Tue–Thu, 7pm–3am Fri & Sat

Step through the doorway of this low-lit cocktail bar and be transported to another age. With its gleaming wood and chrome, Art Deco-style lamps and curving lemon-coloured armchairs, Ginger is reminiscent of a saloon in a luxurious ocean liner of the 1930s. It's easy to imagine Fred and Ginger at the sinuous bar, perched on the tall chrome-and-leather bar stools, or lounging in one of the numerous nooks and crannies linked by a series of staircases and galleries.

Unusually for a Barcelona cocktail bar, Ginger also offers an excellent range of upmarket tapas (served until 1am). Try a warm salad with grilled camembert, Thai-style stuffed mushrooms, or *botifarra* (Catalan sausage) flambéed in Orujo. The cocktail list includes a delicious Ginger Pimms – perfect on a hot summer's evening. There is also a good range of wines and cavas, including a fruity cava tinta (red cava).

Bars & Clubs

La Palma *old-fashioned bodega-bar* `6 E4`
C/Palma de Sant Just 7 • 93 315 0656
Open 8am–3:30pm and 7–10pm daily (to 11 Fri & Sat)

Time has stood still in this sleepy bodega, with its battered wooden tables, hanging hams, yellowing walls and lazy paddle fans. It's stacked with huge barrels full of a potent local wine, served up in thick terracotta jugs along with Catalan staples like cured meats and *pa amb tomaquet* (tomato-rubbed bread).

Pilé 43 *retro furniture and cocktails* `5 C4`
C/N'Aglà 4 • 93 317 3902
Open 7pm–2am Mon–Sat

Bright, funky Pilé 43 is tucked away down a hard-to-find alley, but it's worth the effort to seek out. The place is coolly decorated with a mix of retro furniture. Perch on a 50s-style bar stool, or sink into a lurid 70s couch. And, if you like what you see, take it home with you – everything is for sale.

Pipa Club *classic last-drink spot* `5 C4`
Plaça Reial, principal 3 • 93 302 4732
 www.bpipaclub.com Open 10pm–3am daily

By day, the Pipa Club is a members-only bar dedicated to pipe-smokers. But, after 10pm, everyone is made welcome to the cosy, English-style snug bar and wood-panelled lounge – just ring the bell and go on up. Overlooking the buzzy square, the club packs out late with students and arty locals.

Club 13 *slinky restaurant-club* `5 C4`
Plaça Reial 13 • 93 317 2352
Open restaurant: 8:30pm–midnight Sun–Thu,
8:30pm–1am Fri & Sat; club: 11pm–3am daily

One of a new breed of restaurant-bar-clubs that has mushroomed across the city, Club 13 covers all bases. Sprawl languidly on Moroccan-style beds and sample excellent Mediterranean cuisine, then descend to the basement, where DJs spin hip-hop and electronica.

Jamboree *jazz, flamenco and DJs* `5 C4`

Plaça Reial 17 • 93 319 1789
» www.masimas.com/jamboree
Open 10:30pm–5:30am daily

Right on Plaça Reial in the heart of the old city's main nightlife district, Jamboree is probably Barcelona's best-known jazz venue. Set in atmospheric, brick-lined cellars surrounding the stage, the bar is hung with striking black-and-white photographs of some of the big-name performers who have headlined here.

Upstairs, you'll find Tarantos, one of the city's few flamenco venues. It may be a tad touristy, but the dancers and musicians are among the best around. The jazz club and flamenco *tablao* have separate admission fees but, after the sessions have finished, the spaces are joined to become a nightclub. The dancing keeps going until dawn, with upbeat Latin and salsa rhythms upstairs, and DJ Yoda's selection of funk and hip-hop downstairs. Popular with tourists, Jamboree also attracts a massive crowd of regulars.

Júpiter *relaxed hang-out* `6 E4`

C/Jupi 4 • 93 268 3650
» www.jupiteryluna.com Open 7pm–1 Tue–Sun (to 2 Fri & Sat)

This is a welcoming gay-run bar, with cheerfully mis-matched sofas and walls crammed with art. Good for tea and cakes before 9pm, it's also perfect for cocktails and beer later on. You can dine simply on home-made pasta and salads here, or at their restaurant (La Luna de Júpiter) round the corner on pretty Plaça Traginers.

Las Cuevas del Sorte *café-bar* `6 E4`

C/Gignás 2 • 93 318 7913
Open 7pm–2:30am Wed–Mon (to 3am Fri & Sat)

Jim and Sulin transformed this former transvestite flamenco *tablao* into a magical, whitewashed grotto, with shimmering walls, columns and tables of pale Gaudí-esque shattered ceramics. There are two bars for wine and cocktails, one of them in the basement, where plays and live music are occasionally performed.

Bars & Clubs

Borneo *mellow bar*
`6 G4`

C/Rec 49 • 93 268 2389

>> www.barborneo.com Open 8pm–3am daily

Grab a table by the huge windows at this intimate, low-lit café-bar and watch the fashionable crowds flow along the Passeig del Born. Relax with a cocktail, a glass of wine (lots to choose from) or tea from the extensive list. Extra stimulation is provided by art exhibitions and wall projections.

Fluxia *New York grooves*
`6 G3`

Passeig de Picasso 20 • 67 536 0189 (mobile)

Open 8pm–2am Wed–Sun (to 3am Fri & Sat)

A gorgeous hot-pink cavern run by charismatic Brooklynite Omar, Fluxia offers a taste of New York in the Born. The sounds, played out by DJ Jimmy Chicago, run from NY soul to electro-funk. Benches for lounging on, a great cocktail list, and the eclectic crowd make this a fabulous place to start the night.

Flow *hip chill-out lounge*
`6 G4`

C/Fusina 6 • 93 310 0667

Open 8pm–3am Tue–Sun

Effortlessly glamorous, this designer lounge-bar offers excellent cocktails. Mixologist Lorena makes the best Cosmopolitan in Barcelona, while the house speciality is a tongue-tingling frozen Mojito. Rippling projections, loungey chill-out music, low leather seating and mood lighting keep the vibe laid-back yet upbeat.

Gimlet *sophisticated cocktail bar*
`6 G4`

C/Rec 24 • 93 310 1027

Open 8pm–3am Mon–Sat

The classiest bar in the fashionable Born, Gimlet serves expertly mixed cocktails (including a fine version of the eponymous vodka concoction) to Barcelona's theatre and film crowd. Chrome stools are lined against the smooth curve of the polished bar, and a soothing, jazzy soundtrack adds sophistication.

Pitín Bar *classic neighbourhood café-bar* `6 F4`
Passeig del Born 34 • 93 319 5087
>> www.pitinbar.com Open 6pm–2am Mon–Thu, 6pm–3am Fri, 11pm–3am Sat, 11am–midnight Sun

This long-standing veteran was here well before the Born became the hottest nightlife district in the city, and its effortless cool makes many an over-designed neighbour green with envy. The small downstairs bar area has a simple 50s-style counter bar, with another stretched along a huge window, from which you can gaze out at the fashionable crowds.

Upstairs, a cosy, low-ceilinged salon is draped with velvet curtains and scattered with vintage typewriters, battered old mirrors and all manner of knick-knacks. Here you can enjoy the Pitín's unusual speciality: tea made like a cappuccino, with a cloud of frothy milk. To go with it, try the delicious sandwiches and cakes (the brownies are especially good). Best of all, though, is the huge outdoor terrace – a prime people-watching position at the top of the Passeig del Born.

Plàstic Café *retro-kitsch disco bar* `6 F4`
Passeig del Born 19 • 93 310 2596
Open 10pm–2:30am Tue–Thu & Sun, 10pm–3am Fri & Sat

The funky, fashionable Plàstic Café, with its weird, underlit orange bar and kitsch baubles, packs out with local fashionistas, students, tourists and anyone else looking for a good, fun time. The tiny dance floor is crammed at weekends, as DJs pump out funk, house and dance to an always up-for-it crowd.

L'Hivernacle de la Ciutadella `6 H3`
Passeig de Picasso s/n • 93 295 4017
Open 9am–midnight Mon–Sat, 9am–5pm Sun

For a break from the Born's hyper-fashionable bars, try this airy, palm-filled 19th-century greenhouse in the lovely Parc de la Ciutadella *(see p143)*. An informal, traditional café-bar, Hivernacle is a relaxing place for a coffee or snack by day, and offers a great programme of live jazz during the summer *(see p97)*.

Repùblica *subterranean nightclub* `6 G5`
Estació de França, Avinguda Marquès de l'Argentera 6
Open 1am–7am Fri & Sat

A cavernous club underneath the França train station, Repùblica is where trendy young Barcelonins dance frenetically to thudding electro-dance music, and metrosexuals pose in the slick white chill-out zone. A smaller, purple-lit dance floor is dedicated to poppier sounds for the more fun-loving clubber.

El Café Que Pone Muebles `5 A1`
Navarro *sofas and cocktails*
C/Riera Alta 4–6
Open 6pm–1am Tue–Sun (to 2:30am Fri & Sat)

The kitschy leopard-skin and fake-leather sofas in this airy café-bar are all left over from the premises' former incarnation as a furniture shop. Sunny yellow walls keep it bright, and there are snacks (pricey) to go with the drinks. Good for chilling on Sundays.

Aurora *tiny boho-chic bar* `5 A2`
C/Aurora 7 • 93 442 3044
Open 8pm–2:30am daily (to 3am Fri & Sat)

Psychedelic colours swirl across every inch of this tiny neighbourhood bar, where boho-chic locals sprawl around groovy plastic tables or lounge on cool flea-market finds. Mellow to start, Aurora packs out late, when the chill-out music gives way to funkier electronic sounds. Closing times are fluid.

Bar Pastís *classic French-style bar* `5 B4`
C/Santa Mònica 4 • 93 318 7980
Open 7:30pm–2:30pm Tue–Sun (to 3:30am Fri & Sat)

The brothels and cabarets may have vanished from the Raval, but some things remain the same and this charismatic bar is little changed since it opened in 1947. Where once it served pastis to homesick French sailors, it now draws an eclectic crowd of nostalgia-seekers and the occasional transvestite.

La Confitería café-bar for a tête-à-tête `5 A3`
C/Sant Pau 128 • 93 443 0458
Open 7pm–3am Mon–Sat, 7pm–2am Sun

Set in a former Modernista bakery – complete with burnished mirrors, glittering chandeliers and swirling woodwork – La Confitería is a tranquil café-bar that serves a good range of wines, along with teas, coffees and standard bar drinks. Relaxing and low-key, it's a good place for catching up with friends.

Benidorm hip local for lovers of kitsch `5 B1`
C/Joaquín Costa 39 • 93 317 8052
Open 8pm–2:30am daily (to 3am Fri & Sat)

From the blown-up 70s-style postcard of the infamous resort that serves as the bar sign, to the flock wallpaper and disco-ball that glitters over the miniature dance floor, Benidorm is a temple to kitsch. Both the music (everything from chill-out to electro-dance) and the crowd are hip and groovy.

Ambar sofas and DJs `5 B3`
C/Sant Pau 77
Open 6pm–2am daily (to 3am Fri & Sat)

This relaxed café-bar has a great terrace for warm evenings. The funky retro-pop interior has cosy, mismatched sofas, colourful lights and a slick red bar. Relax over an early-evening coffee or a snack, or a cocktail later on. The atmosphere is far buzzier at the weekend, when DJs ensure that the place is crammed.

Great Bars for Tapas

Elegant **Ginger** *(see p111)* serves sophisticated tapas to go with its excellent selection of wines and cavas. For perfectly prepared Catalan delicacies, such as *botifarra amb mongetes* (Catalan sausage with white beans), try stylish little **Mam i Teca** (C/Lluna 4; Map 5 A1) or the Gothic stone interior of **Va de Ví** (C/Banys Vells 16; Map 6 F4) for cured meats and pungent cheeses. Old-fashioned, colourfully tiled **El Xampanyet** (C/Montcada 22; Map 6 F3), is a classic serving cava and chunks of *bacallà* (salt cod). The standing-room-only, bottle-lined bodega **Quimet & Quimet** (C/Poeta Cabanyes; Map 3 D3) is a fabulous neighbourhood favourite in Poble Sec, with an enormous selection of wines to go with its upmarket, original tapas.

>> *For a selection of the city's best restaurants serving tapas, see p27*

Bars & Clubs

Marsella *Barcelona's oldest bar* `5 B3`
C/Sant Pau 65 • 93 442 7263
Open 6pm–2:30am Mon–Thu, 6pm–3am Fri & Sat

The aroma of absinthe wafts through the air in Barcelona's oldest bar – a faded beauty, crammed with bottle-filled cabinets, chandeliers, battered marble-topped tables and mirrors bearing slogans for long-defunct products. The "green fairy" is still drunk here in the traditional way – through a sugar cube.

La Paloma *opulent club setting* `4 E1`

C/Tigre 27 • 93 301 6897
» www.lapaloma-bcn.com
Open midnight–5am Thu, 2–5am Sat & Sun

A plush, gilded theatre is the surprising venue for one of the best club nights in the city – Thursday's Bongo Lounge, run by the fabulous Dope Brothers. Other club nights take over on Fridays and Saturdays. The theatre is used for ballroom dancing before midnight.

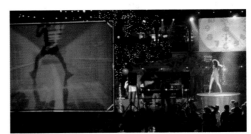

La Concha `5 B4`
C/Guardia 14 • 93 302 4118
Open 5pm–2:30am Sun–Thu, 5pm–3am Fri & Sat

This bar is a temple to sultry singing star of the 1950s and 60s Sara Montiel. The walls are papered with photographs of the iconic chanteuse, and La Concha is one of the few places where traces of the old louche Raval still linger. At weekends, you can dance to Spanish pop on a tiny dance floor.

Madame Jasmine *cool meets kitsch* `5 A3`
Rambla del Raval 22
Open 9am–1am Sun–Thu, 9am–3am Fri & Sat

A cosy bar that caters for a diverse crowd, Madame Jasmine serves snacks by day and killer cocktails by night. The atmosphere is a mix of cool and kitsch, with recycled decor that weaves between trendy bar and your granny's living room. French *chanson*, Latin beats and dance music provide the background vibe.

Jazz Sí Club *live music joint* `5 A1`
C/Requesens 2, off C/Riera Alta • 93 329 0020
» www.tallerdemusics.com Open 9am–11pm Mon–Fri, 6–11pm Sat & Sun; live music 8–10pm

A scruffy, atmospheric club down a back street in the Raval, Jazz Sí Club is part of the Barcelona music school and offers a nightly programme of live gigs for a studenty crowd. Jazz jam sessions are on Wednesdays, flamenco on Fridays and rock on Saturdays.

Zentraus Dance Club *electronica* `5 A3`
Rambla del Raval 41 • 93 443 8078
>> www.zentraus.com
Open 9pm–2:30am Tue–Thu, 9pm–3am Fri & Sat

Though a newcomer to the increasingly hip Rambla del Raval, Zentraus is easily one of the best clubs in the city. Small and sleek in red and black, it has a loungey seating area, with cushioned stools set around inner-lit tables, and an amazing creamy bar that's also lit from within. The place is run by music-mad Morello, a passionate aficionado of electronic music. He ensured that the very best sound system was installed, and invites top local and international DJs to the turntables. Zentraus is cool without being pretentious, the music is fantastic and the crowd is friendly and enthusiastic. Different nights bring different inflections of techno, electro, drum 'n' bass and breakbeat, while flickering projections animate the small dance floor. Weekends are busy, but mid-week this is an excellent place for a pre-club drink.

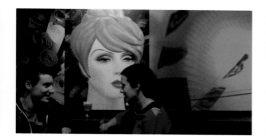

Zelig *live music and snacks* `5 A2`
C/Carme 116 • 64 926 1599
>> www.zelig-barcelona.com
Open 7pm–2am Tue–Sun (to 3am Fri & Sat)

Gay-owned and gay-friendly, Zelig nevertheless attracts a mixed (gay and straight) crowd of hip young locals and international visitors. Its formula of reasonably priced snacks and drinks, live music and sleek decor has made it an instant hit in the Raval.

Metro *gay nirvana* `4 E1`
C/Sepúlveda 185 • 93 323 5227
>> www.metrodiscobcn.com
Open midnight–late Mon–Sat, 1am–late Sun

Metro takes you into a subterranean world, with small, intimately lit spaces, two dance floors and a "dark room". Lose yourself to the hard, energetic vibe in Sala 1, or dance to happy Spanish pop in Sala 2. Every night has a different theme, from cabaret to bingo.

Salvation *one for the boys* `3 D2`
Ronda de Sant Pere 19–21 • 93 318 0686
>> www.matineegroup.com Open midnight–6am Fri & Sat

This classic gay disco is for men only (women need
to arrange entrance in advance), and attracts a
beautiful, buffed crowd. With pumping house on one
dance floor, gay anthems on the other, hot bar staff
and nightly shows, Salvation has established itself
as a major club on Barcelona's gay scene.

Sala Apolo *hedonistic nightclub* `3 D3`
C/Nou de la Rambla 113 • 93 441 4001
>> www.sala-apolo.com Open Nitsa: 12:30–6:30am Fri & Sat;
Powder Room: 12:30–6am Thu

Set in a huge, refurbished theatre (the Sala Apolo),
the excellent Nitsa Club gets a happy crowd pumping
to the latest electro-dance music, funk, breaks and
rare groove. On Thursdays, Powder Room takes over:
a major gay club night that packs the dance floor.

Barcelona Rouge *candle-lit cocktail bar* `3 D3`
C/Poeta Cabanyes 21 • 93 442 4985
Open 11pm–late (approx 2:20am during the week,
3 or 4am at weekends) Tue–Sat

A cross between a boudoir and someone's eccentric
living-room, Barcelona Rouge is a welcoming, candle-
lit space with intimate corners, plump sofas scattered
with silk cushions and walls adorned with colourful
murals. Red, of course, is the dominant theme, with
soft red lighting and a deliberately cultivated louche
ambience, reminiscent of Parisian bars of the 1950s.

The bold murals are the work of Carme, who, along
with co-owner Thomas, set up the bar in 1996. The
music is chilled-out and atmospheric – French
chanteuses alternate with Brazilian rhythms. The
friendly clientele is a mixed bag, with middle-aged
locals and hip young couples coming here to sip
cocktails. There's an extensive list but, if daunted,
opt for the house speciality, Rouge Punch, which is
made with an excellent Martinique rum.

Discothèque *club for beautiful people* `3 A1`
Poble Espanyol • 93 511 5764
>> www.discotheque.es
Open midnight–6am Fri & Sat

A stalwart of the Barcelona clubbing scene, glamorous Discothèque attracts top international DJs. A fashionable crowd packs the floor, dancers slink around on podiums and massive projections whirl overhead. A smaller space is dedicated to hip-hop and R&B.

CDLC (Carpe Diem Lounge Club) `4 H5`
Passeig Marítim 32 • 93 224 0470
>> www.cdlcbarcelona.com Open noon–3am daily

Only steps from the beach, CDLC oozes languid elegance. Even the outdoor terrace is kitted out with multi-coloured carpets, gilded armchairs and Balinesian-style cushioned bed areas for relaxation at its most decadent. The restaurant serves decent Mediterranean and fusion dishes, but CDLC really comes into its own as a nightclub.

The huge club boasts discreet VIP lounges, dripping with Moroccan-style beaded lights and piled high with silk cushions, and slightly less ostentatious areas for regular clubbers – sprawl on vast cushioned beds and watch the beautiful crowd, while diaphanous curtains billow around you. The dance floor is always crammed, thanks to some of the best DJs in the city, and each night offers a different genre. On Sunday nights in summer, the party heads to the beach, with performances by fire-jugglers and acrobats.

Barceloneta's Neighbourhood Bars
Old-fashioned and endearingly shabby, Barceloneta is one of the best places for a tapas crawl. **El Vaso de Oro** (C/Balboa 6; Map 4 H4) is revered for its beer and excellent tapas, heaped high on a long, narrow bar. **Can Ramonet** (C/Maquinista 17; Map 4 H4) is the oldest tavern in the barri. It serves great seafood tapas, which are eaten at stools around huge barrels, and has a posher restaurant attached. Scruffy, workers' favourite **Can Ganassa** (Plaça de la Barceloneta; Map 4 G4) has a terrace on a pretty square, and serves Catalan favourites such as *torrades* (toasted country bread with fresh toppings). Boho-chic **Daguiri** (C/Grau i Torras, off C/Sant Carles; Map 4 G5) has international papers and magazines, and a perfect seafront location.

Bars & Clubs

Sal Café *cool beachside restaurant-bar* `4 H5`
Passeig Marítim s/n • 93 224 0707
Open noon–5pm and 8:30pm–1am Tue–Sun (to 3am Thu–Sat)

This fashionable bar-restaurant has a fantastic beach-front location. Once diners have feasted on excellent contemporary Mediterreanean cuisine (on the terrace or in the orange-and-black retro interior), DJs take to the decks, playing smooth lounge and chill-out as the stylish crowd sips cocktails and watches the waves.

Space *stunning new mega-club* `1 A5`
C/Tarragona 141-7 • 93 426 8444
>> www.spacebarcelona.com
Open midnight–6am Fri & Sat

One of the newest and coolest clubs in the city, this vast underground space is the place to go and lose it on the dance floor. Resident and guest DJs play the newest house and techno-house, and the massive dance floor seethes with trendy young Barcelonins.

Antilla BCN Latin Club *sultry sounds* `1 B5`
C/Aragó 141 • 93 451 4564
>> www.antillasalsa.com
Open 11pm–4am daily (to 5:30am Fri & Sat)

For the hottest Latin and Caribbean sounds, head for Antilla, one of the best and longest-established *salsa-tecas* in Barcelona. Decorated in fabulously over-the-top Caribbean style (complete with palm trees), the club offers fantastic live music and free salsa lessons.

City Hall *varied club nights* `2 E5`
Rambla de Catalunya 2–4
Open midnight–6am daily

Once the lights go down at this city-centre theatre, it reopens as a slick nightclub. Every night is different: electro-house on Tuesdays; electro-clash sessions on Wednesdays; soul and hip-hop on Thursdays; electro-dance kicks in on Fridays; and the week rounds off with house and techno on Saturdays and Sundays.

La Bodegueta del Xampú *cava bar* `2 F5`
Gran Via de les Corts Catalanes 702 • 93 265 0483
Open 8am–1am Mon–Sat

This quiet little neighbourhood bar is a good place to munch on delicious *montaditos* (crusty bread with sophisticated toppings) along with a glass of cava from an extensive list. Scattered with candle-lit tables, the bar is friendly and unpretentious. If you like what you're drinking, pick up a bottle in the adjoining deli.

La Fira *dodgems and carousels* `1 C4`
C/Provença 171
Open 10pm–3am Tue–Sun (to 4:30am Fri & Sat)

Antique fairground attractions are crammed into this weird and wonderful bar in the Eixample. Clamber into a dodgem, perch on a carousel horse, gaze into a distorting mirror, or have your fortune read by a shadowy stranger. And don't be surprised to find a "Groucho Marx" or "Charlie Chaplin" on the tiny dance floor.

Mond Club (in the Club Fellini) `4 F3`
Las Ramblas 27 • 68 796 9825
» www.mondclub.com Open 12:30am–6am Fri

On the last Thursday of the month, the Mond Bar *(see p126)* takes over the Club Fillini theatre for a special night. Living out the Mond Bar motto, "Pop Will Make Us Free", students and hip young things groove to the newest and funkiest pop and electro-disco, courtesy of guest and resident DJs.

Café del Sol *bohemian café-bar* `2 F2`
Plaça del Sol 16 • 93 415 5663
Open noon–2am daily (to 3am Fri & Sat)

Boasting a fabulous terrace right on Gràcia's liveliest square, Café del Sol is an arty little spot. During the day, serious young intellectuals and aesthetes lazily nibble simple tapas and sip cold beer, but at night it gets busier and buzzier. A piano on a gallery level provides the focus for live music on Sunday afternoons.

Bars & Clubs

La Baignoire *laid-back cocktail bar* `2 F2`
C/Verdi 6
Open 7pm–2am daily (to 3am Fri & Sat)

Hang out at the bar while La Baignoire's delightful French owner, Cedric, mixes up a cocktail, then chill out to the mellow sounds. The place is decked out with glistening chandeliers and gilded wallpaper, making it cosy in winter, while the entire glass front can be opened up to create an airy terrace in summer.

Mond Bar *tiny trendy bar* `2 F2`
Plaça del Sol 21 • 93 457 3877
» www.mondclub.com
Open 8:30pm–3am daily

Cool and edgy, this slip of a bar is papered with huge posters advertising Barcelona club nights. Trendy young things lounge in the bench-lined lower room, eerily lit with ultra-violet, while the music ranges from angsty pop to electro. For the club night, *see p125*.

Sol de Nit *arty bar with terrace* `2 F2`
Plaça del Sol 9–10 • 93 237 3937
Open noon–2:30am daily (to 3am Fri & Sat)

Much loved by arty Gràciencs, this corridor-like bar is an institution on the Plaça del Sol. It's surprisingly cosy and characterful, with beaded chandeliers and swirling suns on well-worn table tops. On sunny afternoons, however, the terrace is the place to be. There are art exhibitions and occasional live gigs too.

Elephant *oriental glamour*
Passeig Til.lers (off Avinguda de Pedralbes) • Palau Reial metro
» www.elephantbcn.com   Open 11:30pm–4.30am Wed–Sun

Seductive and gorgeously over the top, Elephant is an oriental fantasy made real. Lounge on beds in the garden, amid stone elephants and trickling water features, or hit the open-air dance floor. Alternatively, laze in a hammock in an upstairs salon of the mansion. Truly bizarre. Check website for seasonal variations.

Oven *hip restaurant and lounge bar* `7 B3`
C/Ramón Turró 126, Poblenou • 93 221 0602
Open 9pm–3am Thu–Sat

A single blue light above an unpromising archway is all that announces this bar and restaurant, hidden down an eerily quiet street in Poblenou. But Oven has no problem pulling in the punters, and is one of the hottest places in town. Hard-edged industrial chic meets lounge-style glamour in this stunning converted warehouse. Slinky red sofas are gathered round low tables, bold contemporary art is dotted about and enormous globe lights hang from high ceilings.

A cinder-block wall studded with candles stretches back to the informal dining area, where a short but excellent menu of inventive fusion cuisine is served. Behind the long bar, genial bartenders shake up excellent cocktails (including fabulous Mojitos) and, as the night wears on, some of the best DJs in the city spin breakbeat and funk. In summer, book well in advance for a candlelit table on the terrace.

Mirablau *best city views*
Plaça Doctor Andreu 1 • 93 418 5879 • Pl del Funicular metro
Open 11am–4:30am daily (to 5:30am Fri & Sat)

This simple café-bar is set halfway up the Tibidabo mountain and offers staggering views over the entire city, all the way down to the sea. Downstairs, a cheery club gets going late on, with a mix of commercial pop and favourites from the 60s and 70s. In summer, a glorious garden and terrace are opened up.

Danzatoria *spectacular restaurant-club*
Avinguda Tibidabo 61 • 93 272 0040 • Pl del Funicular metro
» www.gruposalsitas.com Open restaurant: 9pm–midnight Tue–Sat; club: 11pm–2:30am Tue–Sat

A magnificent early 20th-century mansion perched on the side of the Tibidabo mountain is the spectacular setting for an excellent restaurant-cum-club. There are two dance spaces (one for electro, one for hip-hop) and, in summer, a palm-filled garden is opened up.

streetlife

The famous Boqueria on Las Ramblas is familiar to many visitors, but Barcelona has a wealth of lesser-known but equally colourful markets in areas such as seaside Barceloneta and laid-back Gràcia. Elsewhere in the city, you can soak up the multi-ethnic atmosphere of the Raval, head for the time-warp barri of Sant Pere, or make a day-trip to Sitges – the winter weekend retreat and ultimate summertime party town.

Streetlife

Plaça del Rei *sublime Gothic ensemble* `6 E3`

Regal Plaça del Rei (King's Square) is hemmed in by a crowd of Gothic buildings that provides a theatrical backdrop for a picnic, an outdoor concert, or the serenades of a passing street musician. Dominated by the austere **Palau Reial** (Royal Palace) and adjoining chapel – where, for centuries, the rulers of Catalunya held court and prayed – the square oozes history from every stone. And, indeed, beneath the medieval stones lie the ancient ruins of Roman Barcino, which are still astonishingly intact. Peek in the glass windows on adjoining Carrer del Veguer to glimpse them, or study them more carefully as part of a visit to the fascinating **Museu d'Història de la Ciutat** *(see p78)*. The museum now incorporates the Royal Palace, the **Royal Chapel** and the **Roman ruins**. The Royal Chapel has a dainty bell tower, with a delicate, wrought-iron crown; it contrasts somewhat with the

grim **Mirador del Rei Martí** – a watchtower built to keep an eye on the overly independent Catalans.

In the square itself, locals walk their dogs, kids career past on their way back from school, and footsore tourists sprawl on the magnificent steps that sweep up to the Royal Palace. These steps form a dramatic natural stage for frequent outdoor summer concerts, particularly during the excellent **Festival de Música Antigua** (Festival of Early Music; *see p16*).

In summer, a terrace café, **L'Antiquari de la Plaça del Rei**, has tables spread out across the square, while street performers regale the drinkers with everything from sentimental ballads to tango dances or fire-breathing tricks. The boxy public sculpture by Eduardo Chillida serves as an impromptu stage for such performances. At night, the square is even more enchanting, with starlight gleaming palely overhead, and music echoing off the ancient walls.

Las Ramblas *celebrated city promenade* `5 C2`

Boqueria market: 8am–8:30pm Mon–Sat
Arts and crafts market: 10am–6pm daily (to 10pm in summer)

The mile-long series of avenues that forms Las Ramblas, the city's most famous promenade, sweeps in a seamless procession through the Old City en route to the harbour. Hang around long enough, and all humanity seems to pass this way: dazed tourists, trolley-wielding grandmothers, opera singers and human statues.

Each of the five avenues that make up Las Ramblas has a distinct personality. The **Rambla de las Canaletes** is named after a florid fountain: drink from this, says the legend, and you'll return to Barcelona. On the **Rambla dels Ocells** ("of the birds") you can pick up a canary or a hamster from one of several pet shops, and on the **Rambla de les Flors**, you can choose a

fresh bouquet from a perfumed stall. Modernista monuments are clustered here too, including the gilded **Escribà Patisserie** (No. 83) and the striking former umbrella shop **Casa Bruno Quadros** (No. 82), with its parasol-toting dragon. Most famous of all is the **Boqueria** (www.boqueria.info), Barcelona's biggest food market, with colourful stalls of wet fish, succulent fruit, cured meats and oven-fresh bread.

The celebrated **Gran Teatre del Liceu** *(see p96)* regally surveys the **Rambla de las Caputxins,** and the elegant **Café de l'Òpera** opposite has a great people-watching terrace. Only one sex shop has held out on the once-seedy **Rambla de Santa Mònica,** where an arts and crafts market now holds sway. The terrace-café at the **Centre d'Art Santa Mònica** (No. 7) is another superb spot for surveying the human tide.

>> *Housed in a former convent, the Centre d'Art Santa Mònica hosts exhibitions of contemporary and Catalan art* `131`

Streetlife

Carrer Sant Pere mes Baix 6 F2

Escape Barcelona's obsession with style and design in this resolutely old-fashioned shopping street in the heart of the time-warp barrio of Sant Pere. Among the traditional grocers, fishmongers and bakeries are some Modernista architectural gems, such as pretty **Farmacia Fonoll** at No. 52, with its beautiful stained glass and extraordinary wrought-iron chandelier. Faded sgraffito decoration still adorns some of the street's oldest façades. Neighbours gather at street corners and musty shop counters to gossip, and shop windows offer decidedly unglamorous goods, from sensible knickers to orthopedic shoes.

The occasional snatch of salsa music drifts from open windows where South American immigrants have made their home, but change is palpably in the air. The opening of the stunning covered market of **Santa Caterina,** with its undulating mosaic roof, and a cautious sprinkling of new galleries and fashionable bars are intimations of creeping gentrification.

Passeig del Born *fashionable boulevard* 6 F4

This is the main drag of the ultra-hip Born neighbourhood, overlooked by the sublime cathedral of **Santa María del Mar,** and lined with trees and benches. Pull up a chair at one of the terrace cafés and watch the fashionable crowds sway past, or browse through the quirky shops selling everything from interior design to cheeses. Look out for **Czar** *(see p62)*, which does a nice line in cool and wacky footwear.

Rambla del Poblenou *old charmer* 7 D2

The old-fashioned seaside neighbourhood of Poblenou has its very own Rambla – a tranquil, tree-lined avenue sprinkled with Modernista mansions and lined with seating. Here, elderly locals come to take a seat and watch the world go by. Pop into **El Tio Che** (Nos. 44–6; www.eltioche.com) for refreshment. It has been serving the best ice-cold *orxata* (a creamy, nutty drink) in the city since 1912, and the locals love it.

Barceloneta *community charm*   `4 G5`

Market: Open 7am–2pm Mon–Thu,
7am–2pm & 4:30–8pm Fri, 7am–3pm Sat

Tucked in the shadows of the glitzy and more glamorous Port Vell and Passeig Marítim, life goes on in the refreshingly old-fashioned neighbourhood of Barceloneta much as it has for generations. Traditionally home to fishermen and dock workers, it has remained impervious to the design fever that has taken over much of the rest of the city, and is still scattered with resolutely old-fashioned tapas bars and cafés that haven't changed in decades.

Built in the 18th century on reclaimed land, Barceloneta – a tidy grid of narrow streets set around airy squares – was one of the first planned neighbourhoods in the city. But restrictions on building heights were soon ignored, and the narrow streets quickly closed in as buildings got higher and higher. These gully-like streets, with their flapping lines of washing and wrought-iron balconies, now frame enticing glimpses of the palm trees lining the sea front, or waves crashing on the beach. At the annual **Festa Major** in late September and early October *(see p18)*, they are covered with eccentric canopies (formed by strings of cans, bunting, tinsel and all kinds of recycled junk), while snack stalls and stages are set up beneath. This fabulous festival is the best time to visit the humble barri, when its community spirit and ramshackle charm are most evident.

The heart of Barceloneta, as in most of Barcelona's traditional neighbourhoods, is the **market,** which is set out on the Plaça de la Font. Piled high with gleaming fish and other fresh produce, it is an excellent spot for buying picnic supplies. Around it is a smattering of traditional bars and cafés, one or two still with sawdust-covered floors. A charming fountain bubbles away in the centre of Plaça de la Barceloneta. Sitting prettily on the square is the little Baroque church of **Sant Miquel** and an excellent, earthy tapas bar, **Can Ganassa** *(see p123)*, which has a big summer terrace.

>> *For more about Barceloneta's local bars,* see p123

133

Rambla del Raval   *vibrant hang-out*   `5 A3`

A few years ago, this area of the Raval was a grubby and dangerous warren of dark alleys lined with rotting tenements. The city decided to rip the whole lot down and replace it with a shiny new promenade, opening up the heart of the neighbourhood, and filling it with palm trees and benches. It's taken a couple of years for the Rambla del Raval to knit in with its surroundings, but – now that terrace cafés have spread out their tables, and the trees are taller and leafier – it is finally beginning to look more at home. It will soon seem more so, as construction work is about to end on one side, with work complete on a new hotel, office and housing complex.

The promenade displays Barcelona at its most multicultural: knots of Indians and North Africans gather to chat, and families picnic on the benches.

Local kids kick footballs, and race up and down, totally absorbed in games of tag.

Students and arty locals hang out in trendy new bars and cafés, such as the funky retro-style **Ambar** *(see p117)* and the pretty little **Café de les Delicies** at No. 47. Arguably, this café serves the best teas in the city. Another feature of the Rambla del Raval is Fernando Botero's huge sculpture of a cat. Having been shunted all around Barcelona since it arrived in the city in 1987, the feline was finally given a permanent home on the road here. It has proved a hit with the neighbourhood kids, who frequently use it as a climbing frame.

In summer, the road becomes an occasional gig venue, which might be anything from flamenco to rock. These are most frequent during the local festival in mid-July or during La Mercè in September *(see p18)*.

Plaça Vicenç Martorell *family fun* `5 C1`

This attractive little square is shaded by trees and surrounded by narrow, appealingly shabby early 20th-century buildings. The old **Casa de la Misericòrdia** is now an administrative building but, in days gone by, unwanted children were abandoned at its revolving door. Nuns would then collect the children and hang labels around their necks marking the date on which they entered the orphanage.

It's an altogether happier place for children now, with a small playground and lawn, where trendy young families come to hang out on sunny days. Neighbourhood locals sit on the terraces of cool cafés such as **Kasparo** *(see p36)* – which serves good coffee and has the sunniest terrace – and **Oolong**, which does excellent fresh juices and lunch dishes, including a great Oriental soup with noodles and lemon grass. There's even a handy newspaper kiosk at which to pick up something to read over lunch, or you could buy a book at **La Central** *(see p70)*, which also has a café.

Mercat de la Concepció *busy market* `2 F5`

C/Aragó 313–17 • 93 457 5329
» www.laconcepcio.com **Food stalls:** open 8am–3pm Mon, 8am–8pm Tue–Fri, 8am–4pm Sat

The graceful glass and wrought-iron building that houses this market was designed by Antoni Rovira i Trias. It was one of the first structures to be built in the Eixample district when the area was newly laid out in 1888. The market was given a thorough overhaul in 1998, which removed some of its old, battered charm but added much-needed modern amenities.

It is still one of the busiest and least touristy markets in the city. Chatty stallholders are always willing to dispense advice on everything from buying the freshest fish to cooking artichokes perfectly. In the touristy Boqueria *(see p131)*, you need to be wary of scams, but not here, where the traders know all their regulars by name. The market is famous among Barcelonins for its colourful and fragrant flower stalls, which are open 24 hours a day.

Streetlife

Mercat de la Llibertat *locals' market* `2 E2`

Plaça Llibertat 27 • 93 217 0995 Open 7am–2pm Mon, 7am–
2pm & 5–8pm Tue, Wed & Thu, 7am–8pm Fri, 7am–3pm Sat

Funky Gràcia is home to this bustling and colourful
covered market. Built in 1875, it was given a pretty
Modernista roof in 1893 by Francesc Berenguer, one
of Gaudí's most devoted disciples. Just four years
after the market's opening, however, the proud town
of Gràcia was swallowed up by Barcelona. Despite the
encroachment of the city, the resolutely independent
character of the neighbourhood is still discernible in
the market. This is not just in the name ("Liberty
Market"), but also in the strong community
atmosphere found here. Under the wispy wrought-
iron roof, throngs of determined, elderly ladies with
shopping bags on wheels, chefs, families and scruffy
students inspect the heaped displays of fresh
produce. Most will stop for a break at one of the
counter-bar cafés, or at the stall-holders' favourite,
the **Bombay** restaurant at Plaça de la Llibertat 7.

Plaça del Sol *bohemian nightlife* `2 F2`

This tiny square is lined on all sides with bars and
cafés, and in the summer it becomes a sea of terrace
tables. When these fill up (which happens in a flash
on hot summer nights), the steps around the square
become makeshift benches for gatherings of hip
locals, who come to hang out with their friends,
their kids and their pet dogs.

Not particularly beautiful to look at (especially
since it was cemented over to conceal an underground car park), the square has, nonetheless, long
been the focus of Gràcia's cool but down-to-earth
nightlife. Boho-chic cafés such as the **Sol Soler**
(which does excellent tapas), the **Café del Sol** and
Sol de Nit *(see p126)* are still popular after years on
the scene, and newer arrivals such as the **Mond Bar**
(see p126) attract a stylish young crowd.

If you visit the square during Gràcia's neighbourhood festival in August, you'll see it at its most
colourful, with jaunty bunting and hordes of people.

Plaça Major, Vic *medieval market square*

>> www.victurisme.com • Tourist info: 93 886 2091
Vic train station (1hr 20mins from Barcelona's Sants or
Plaça Catalunya stations)

Vic, a handsome and appealing town on a high plain,
is curled around a magnificent square, the Plaça
Major. One of the largest and finest squares in all
Catalunya, Plaça Major was laid out in the Middle
Ages, when Vic was a powerful and prosperous
bishopric. However, the town's origins date back even
further, to a small Roman settlement.

Austere Gothic and Renaissance mansions (such as
Casa Moixó and **Casa Beuló**), elegant Baroque townhouses (**Casa Tolosa**) and fanciful, Modernista concoc-
tions (**Casa Costa** and **Casa Comella**) rub shoulders
above a frill of leaning porticoes. Though not open to
the public, each is marked by a plaque. In summer,
cafés spread out in the square, taking in the sunshine.

The town is celebrated for its traditional market
(Tuesdays and Saturdays), when the square is utterly
transformed, as scores of stall-holders, selling
everything from sausages to stockings, display their
colourful wares, and locals jostle good-naturedly
along the crammed passages. In autumn, look out for
the wonderful mushroom stalls. Catalans are crazy
about wild mushrooms, some of which have startling
names, such as *pet de llop* (wolves' farts) – a non-
edible fungus, in fact – or the tasty *camasec* (dry legs).

Vic is famed for its *embutits* (cured meats),
particularly *llonganissa*, a pungent sausage which
hangs in rosy clumps in dozens of little shops on
and around Plaça Major – try **Salgot**, at No. 14.

In early December, a traditional **medieval market** is
held, with early-music concerts and demonstrations
of ancient crafts, such as pottery and iron-forging.
Best of all is the **Mercat del Ram**, held in the week
before Easter. *Rams* are the elaborate palm crosses
used in Easter Sunday celebrations, and this celebration was first seen here in 875. Parades feature Catalan
gegants and *capgrossos* (giants and fatheads),
castellers build extraordinary human castles, and
stalls sell all kinds of local crafts and fresh produce.

>> *There are plans for a refurbishment of Mercat de la Llibertat, which may cause its temporary closure*

Sitges *winter charm and summer fun*

>> www.sitgestur.com • Sitges station • Cau Ferrat &
Museu Maricel de Mar: C/Fonollar s/n; 93 894 0364
Open summer: 10am–2pm & 5–9pm Tue–Sun; winter: 10am–
1:30pm & 3–6:30pm Tue–Fri, 10am–7pm Sat, 10am–3pm Sun

Undisputed "belle of the coast", Sitges is a delightful,
whitewashed seaside town, wrapped around a rosy
church poised on a promontory. Come in winter, when
the beaches are empty and narrow streets deserted,
and you'll find a dreamy, tranquil spot. In the height
of summer, however, Sitges becomes a hedonistic
fleshpot, packed with trendy Barcelonins, fun-seeking
tourists, and half the gay population of Europe.

The town's reputation for showing the world how
to have a good time goes back to the end of the 19th
century, when Santiago Rusiñol – painter, dilettante
and friend of Picasso – set up home here in a pair of
flamboyantly converted fishermen's cottages. He
filled his abode with paintings, junk and a hoard of
Catalan ironmongery, and called it the **Cau Ferrat**
(Den of Iron). Now, it is a fascinating museum, allied
to next door's **Museu Maricel de Mar**. Museu Maricel
has a collection of paintings spanning 1,000 years,
and frames beautiful sea views through delicate
arches on the top floor. Below it, the enchanting little
Baroque church of **Sant Bartomeu** and **Santa Tecla**
(or "La Punta") is the town's most emblematic sight.

But few come to Sitges for its history: the beaches,
nightlife, and evening fashion parade along the
beachfront promenades, **Passeig de la Ribera** and
Passeig Marítim, are what this town is really about.
Heaving restaurants, hotels, cafés and bars jostle
south in an unbroken line, backing long sandy
beaches that are always packed on summer weekends.

There is a beach populated mostly by gay bathers at the northern end, near the church. And beyond the Hotel Torremar, to the south of the centre, is a mix of gay and nudist beaches. The central beaches cater to everyone else. On the northern side of the church-topped headland is a quiet little bay with another great beach, **Platja de Sant Sebastià**, backed with cafés and traditional restaurants. Beyond it, **Port de Aiguadolç** has a marina edged by gin palaces. Here you can rent boats or jet-skis, and learn to sail or wind-surf.

Good seafront options for lunch or dinner are to be found on Passeig de la Ribera. No. 38 is home to the upmarket **El Velero** (93 894 2051), which offers deliciously fresh seafood, and No. 52 is **La Santa María** (93 894 0999), a traditional favourite.

The narrow, whitewashed streets of the **Old Town** boast plenty of bars, clubs and boutiques, especially along the lively streets of Sant Pau, Sant Pere, Sant Bonaventura and Parellades. For designer clothing for men and women, check out the racks in **Extreme** (C/Parellades 26), or pick up some slinky beachwear at **Oscar** (C/Marqués de Montroig 2). For a cocktail, head down C/1er de Mayo, better known as **Carrer de Pecado** (Sin Street). There, you can stop at the legendary **Parrot Pub** to see divas tottering about on gravity-defying stilettoes, duck into the hip music-bar **Pachito** or watch the crowds flow past from the terrace of the **Montroig Café** (C/Marqués de Montroig 11–13, www.montroigcafe.com).

Sitges has a packed calendar of festivals. Biggest and wildest by far is *carnavales* (carnival), which is held in February or March. It is famous throughout Spain for lavish parades, explosive firework displays and an electric party atmosphere.

havens

For such a compact city, Barcelona is surprisingly green. The slopes of Montjuïc are covered with tranquil, landscaped gardens, while Parc de la Ciutadella spreads out to the east of the Old City. Even in the very centre, there are cloisters, magical squares and intimate tea rooms in which to escape the crowds. Beyond the city boundaries lie wild, mountainous parks, charming medieval towns and sparkling coastal villages.

Havens

6 E3

Plaça Sants Just i Pastor

When the hubbub of the Plaça Sant Jaume gets too much, retreat to this beautiful Gothic square caught in a mesh of shadowy stone alleys. Hemmed in by crooked mansions, and overlooked by the austere but lovely **church of Sants Just i Pastor**, it has a couple of excellent terrace cafés and restaurants, including **Bliss** at No. 4 and **Café de l'Acadèmia** (see p29) for excellent modern Catalan cooking. The church contains a beautiful 16th-century altarpiece and an image of the Madonna of Montserrat (see p148), who made a miraculous appearance here.

Sgraffito garlands swirl over **Palau Moixó**, across the square, and an archway leads to a 15th-century courtyard – part of the **Gallery of Illustrious Catalans**. The gallery is open to visitors for Corpus Christi in mid-June, when you'll be able to see the Catalan tradition of dancing a hollow egg on a fountain. Most days in the square, you'll see dogs slurping at the fountain and kids playing on the church steps.

Plaça de Sant Felìp Neri

5 D3

Tucked away down a hidden alley, Plaça Sant Neri is a quiet and contemplative spot, where the peace is broken only when children from the primary school at the corner erupt from class for their break. Although only a stone's throw from Plaça Nova and the Cathedral, this tiny, magical square is a world away from the relentless crowds and bustle that always threaten to engulf the heart of the Barri Gòtic. At the centre of the square, a fountain tinkles gently, and along one stony flank stands a sleepy church, its façade pocked with bullet holes from the Civil War.

An enormous shoe (originally intended for the Columbus statue in the port) marks the **Museu del Calçat** (open 11am–2pm Tue–Sun; 93 301 4533). Run by the shoemakers' guild, it contains all manner of footwear, including impossibly tiny Baroque slippers. In the evenings, the square becomes a place of silent enchantment, haunted by the occasional lovestruck couple, but more often abandoned to its solitude.

Parc de la Ciutadella *elegant oasis* `6 H4`

This is Barcelona's best-loved city park – a green haven criss-crossed with shady pathways, where picnicking families, bongo-players, lovers and elderly locals come to soak up the sun and enjoy the peace. With its leafy groves and bench-lined paths, it is the perfect city retreat. The ground was once occupied by a fortress, which was demolished in 1869 when the park was laid out. The team of architects responsible for the park's design included the young Gaudí *(see p76)*. Many of the monuments and structures you'll see dotted around are survivors from the Universal Exhibition of 1888; they include Domènech i Montaner's fairy-tale **Castell dels Tres Dragons,** one of the earliest Modernista buildings and now the musty zoology museum. The light-drenched palm-house next door, **L'Hivernacle,** is now a pretty café *(see p115)* that showcases jazz in summer.

In the northwest corner of the park, willow trees droop winsomely over the delightful boating lake, creating a spot that's especially popular for family outings on summer weekends. Overlooking the lake is the extravagant **Cascada**. Gaudí had a hand in the creation of this enormous fountain, which incorporates a grotto surrounded by a cloud of classical deities. Most of the southern end of the park is taken up by Barcelona's **zoo** (www.zoobarcelona.com). Here, an albino gorilla named *Floquet de Neu* (Snowflake) once mugged for the crowds; now it is the turn of his twin baby grandchildren to pose for the cameras.

>> *For information about musical events in Parc de la Ciutadella,* see p97

The Cloister of Sant Pau

5 A4

Carrer de Sant Pau • No telephone
Open 10am–2pm Mon–Sat

Sitting dreamily amid the babble and crowds of the Raval, the lovely Romanesque church of Sant Pau *(see also p84)* was built more than 1,000 years ago on land that then stood far outside Barcelona's old city walls. The simple façade bears a fearsome "Hand of God" carved above the doorway, while palm trees sway loftily overhead.

The tranquil cloister is breathtaking – a miniature beauty, with curving Moorish arches and pairs of slender columns carved with a menagerie of fabulous beasts. Time-worn stone tombs are set into the walls, and just off the cloister is the elaborate 10th-century tombstone of Count Guifré of Borrell (founder of the monastery that once stood here). The simple church, with its honey-coloured walls, is a magical setting for occasional concerts – contact the tourist information office *(see p23)* for performance details.

Salterio   *intimate Mediterranean tea room*

5 D3

Carrer Sant Domènec del Call 4 • 93 302 5028
Open 6pm–1:30am daily

A narrow passage in the old Jewish quarter leads to this intimate little tea room, where locals linger over teas at wooden tables lit with candles and Moroccan-style lanterns. Salterio offers a vast range of teas, but you can't beat the tried-and-tested classic fresh mint tea, especially alongside a honey-drizzled pastry.

Barcelona's Beaches

Barcelona beaches (*platjas* in Catalan) stretch northeast from Barceloneta out beyond Poblenou. **Platja de Sant Sebastià** (Map 4 G5) has a gay and nudist section, but gets more mixed towards **Platja de Barceloneta** (Map 4 H5 & 7 A5). Beyond the bright lights of the Port Olímpic, **Platja de Nova Icàia** (Map 7 C4) is family-oriented.

The restaurants begin to thin out behind trendy **Platja de Bogatell** (Map 7 D5), but *xiringuitos* (snack bars) pump out music and offer snacks throughout the summer. The next beach along, **Platja Mar Bella**, is the best of the lot, with a gay and nudist section at one end, a family-oriented area at the other, and a couple of cool bars in the middle that host summer DJ events and parties (usually Sundays).

Club Natació Atlètic Barceloneta 4 G5

Plaça del Mar s/n • 93 221 0010

>> www.cnab.org Open 6:30am–11pm Mon–Fri, 7am–11pm Sat, 8am–8pm Sun (to 4pm Oct–May)

Situated right on the beach, this is Barcelona's best municipal sports centre. There are classes for tai chi, aerobics and yoga, and facilities include a gym, indoor and outdoor pools (heated in winter), and a wellness centre, with sauna and steam room.

Joan Miró Sculpture Park 3 B3

This small, peaceful garden is half-hidden in a grove of lofty pine trees next to the Fundació Joan Miró (see p87). A geometric pathway picks its way past a handful of striking, weather-worn sculptures by contemporary Catalan artists, including Perejaume and Ernest Altes. Having perused the work, take a seat on the stone bench, and drink in spectacular cityscape views. The garden is open year round, day and night.

Jardins de Laribal *quiet formal gardens* 3 B3

Passeig de Madrona 28 • Info office: 10am–8pm daily (to 6pm Oct–Mar); gardens always open

These leafy, formal gardens spill in gentle terraces down the hillside of Montjuïc, offering beautiful views across the city at every turn. Prettily tiled paths and cascading steps lead through shady groves, past burbling fountains and white-painted bowers that blaze with roses in spring.

At the centre of the park, the immaculately restored villa of **El Font del Gat** gets its name (The Cat's Spring) from a local legend which has it that a cat discovered the nearby spring. The villa was built by eminent Modernista architect Puig i Cadafalch to house a restaurant for the 1929 Universal Exhibition. It now, once again, boasts a delightful place to eat (call 93 289 0404 for reservations), where you can enjoy more fabulous views with your lunch or coffee. The villa is also home to the park information office, which has leaflets detailing all the attractions on Montjuïc.

Havens

Plaça Virreina *village feel*

2 F2

Overlooked by the pretty church of Sant Joan, and flanked on one side by old cottages, this delightful tree-fringed square feels as though it has been transported from a country village. Tables spill onto terraces from a smattering of café-bars, such as the excellent **Virreina Bar**. There, arty locals gather for a quiet drink on sultry summer nights before heading to the nearby **Verdi** arts cinema (www.cines-verdi.com).

Iradier *women's well-being*

C/Iradier 18 • 93 254 1717 • Sarria FGC stop, then 10min walk
>> www.iradier.com
Open 7:45am–10pm Mon–Fri, 11am–7pm Sat & Sun

Catering exclusively to women, Iradier offers every imaginable beauty and health treatment. Besides the usual amenities of pools, gyms and exercise classes, Iradier provides light therapy and infra-red rooms, and a special chamber with oxygenated air.

Jardins de Laberint d'Horta

C/Germans Desvalls s/n • 93 428 3934 • Mundet metro stop
Open 10am–dusk daily

One of the most romantic corners of Barcelona, this spellbinding 18th-century garden is the oldest in the city. It was designed for Joan Antoni Desvalls, Marquis of Llupià and Alfarràs, who introduced the Italian Neo-Classical style to the city. Shady paths lead past enchanting groves, where sculpted nymphs slumber in ivy-draped grottoes and Greek gods gleam palely from marble reliefs or gaze out from miniature temples.

Elegant pavilions and ponds, delicate arbours and impressive fountains appear at every twist and turn, but the star of the show is undoubtedly the exquisite and surprisingly tricky labyrinth, which gives the garden its name. Make it to the languid statue of Eros at the centre, so the story goes, and you'll be lucky in love. The garden's Neo-Classical villa is now an information centre, where you can pick up details about guided tours of the park (Wed & Sun). **Adm**

Parc Natural de Collserola *hillside trails*

Centre d'Informació del Parc, C/Església 92
93 280 3552 • Baixador de Vallvidrera FGC stop
>> www.parccollserola.net
Park information office open 9:30am–3pm daily

The peak of Tibidabo – topped with its Disney-like church and celebrated funfair – is one of Barcelona's best-known attractions. Yet few realize that behind it, stretching along the undulating peaks of the Serra de Collserola, is a beautiful natural park. Forested walking and mountain-biking trails meander past old *masies* (farmhouses), ancient chapels and half-forgotten springs. From there, the pulsing city – just over the hill – seems a world away.

From the station at Baixador de Vallvidrera, stone steps wind up through the woods to the park information office, which has details of local horse-riding facilities, special tours of the park (including occasional star-gazing walks), and maps showing walking and cycling routes. One of the best, if most demanding, hikes culminates at the spellbinding 9th-century **Monastery of Sant Cugat** (open 9:30am–noon and 5pm–8pm daily). Facing the park office, a faded 18th-century **villa** (open 11am–3pm Sat, Sun and public hols except Mondays) now covered in wisteria was once home to Jacint Verdaguer, priest and ardent Catalanist, who wrote the great epic poems *L'Atlàtida* and *Canigó*.

For the sheer exhilarating thrill of it, hire a bike and race down the narrow Carretera de les Aigües, which flanks the mountain-side of Tibidabo and offers tremendous city-wide views.

Garraf Beach *sand, serenity & clear waters*
30min train journey from Barcelona's Sants station to Garraf;
the beach is a 5min walk from Garraf station

When you've had enough of shouldering your way through the masses on the city beaches in Barcelona, jump on a train and head to the enchanting little cove of Garraf. Sheltered by rugged cliffs, and blessed with pristine sands and clear turquoise waters, it is backed with a pretty tumble of whitewashed beach huts. In the height of summer, even this beach is busy, so try to go mid-week or out of season – from October to March it is always quiet and deeply romantic.

Hotel Garraf (www.hotelgarraf.com) overlooks the beach and has a terrace where you can dine on Catalan specialities, including the refreshing and substantial local salad *Xató*. Should you tire of the beach, you can visit a little-known Gaudí monument, Celler Güell – a fantastical interpretation of a medieval castle. It is now an upmarket restaurant called **Gaudí-Garraf** (www.gaudigarraf.com).

Montserrat *sacred peaks and natural park*
FGC train from Plaça Espanya to Montserrat-Aeri (for cable car)
or Monistrol de Montserrat (for rack-and-pinion railway)
>> www.abadiamontserrat.net

The pinnacles of Montserrat have been sacred to the Catalans since the discovery of a miraculous statue of the Madonna in the 9th century. The Benedictine monastery, clamped dramatically to the mountainside ever since, remains a place of pilgrimage, and the Madonna – affectionately known as *La Moreneta* (little brown one) – now resides in the gloomy basilica.

Getting to Montserrat is half the fun of a visit: you can sway across the valley on a heart-stopping cable car, or be cranked up by a rack-and-pinion railway. After paying your respects to *La Moreneta*, abandon the over-commercialized monastery and head for the beautiful natural park. A funicular railway can deposit you at the start of a network of walking trails, which wind past peaks worn smooth by time, and through scrubby forest to tiny, half-forgotten chapels.

Tarragona's Old City *Catalunya's Imperial past*

Regional or high-speed train from Barcelona-Sants to Tarragona
(1hr 10mins or 50mins); then 15min walk to the Old City
>> www.tarragonaturisme.es

As the Roman city of Tarraco, this was one of the most important and splendid cities of Imperial Spain. The old city, hemmed in by remnants of the ancient walls, is still liberally scattered with magnificent Roman ruins, which have been granted World Heritage status by UNESCO. The ancient hub of Tarragona is perched on a hilltop, with commanding views over the coastline, particularly from the **Balcó del Mediterrani** (Balcony of the Mediterranean), which has a bird's-eye view of the Roman amphitheatre.

At the heart of the Old City is the vast early Gothic **Cathedral**. Its oddly truncated towers surround an enchanting cloister with exquisitely carved capitals. **Carrer Cavallers** was the finest address in medieval Tarragona, and is still lined with mouldering Gothic

townhouses, boasting graceful courtyards. At No. 14, **Casa Castellarnau** is now part of the **Museu d'Història de Tarragona** (www.museutgn.com). Another section of the museum – formerly known as Museu Romanitat – is located in a medieval palace, close to Plaça del Rei. It was built on the ruins of a Roman mansion, which is indicative of the layers of history that suffuse Tarragona. Just off Plaça del Rei, the **Museu Nacional Arqueològic** (www.mnat.es) focuses on the earliest part of Tarragona's history, and paints a vivid picture of life in Imperial Tarraco.

Unsurprisingly, **Plaça del Forum** was the location of the Roman provincial forum, and was once fringed with arcades. Of these, a few fragments survive at either end of the square. For spectacular views, head along the **Passeig Arqueològic** – an attractive walkway that winds between the ancient Roman walls and the British-built military fortifications of the 1700s. From here, the surrounding plains are spread before you.

>> *Head up to the roof of the Museu Nacional Arqueològic for more breathtaking views of Tarragona and beyond* 149

hotels

From luxury retreats in Modernista mansions to budget *hostals* on leafy squares, Barcelona has plenty of characterful accommodation. The chic Eixample has most of the cool, stylish hotels, while the Raval and Barri Gòtic boast atmospheric old charmers – from 18th-century palaces to former convents. Beach fans can soak up the view at the spectacular Hotel Arts, and shopaholics should consider hotels in the fashionable Born.

HOTELS

Barcelona must have the greatest concentration of "design hotels" in any European city. Some of these are truly outstanding and offer cutting-edge interiors, world-class pampering and superb gastronomy. Accommodation in the moderate price range has traditionally been a bit dull, but things have changed considerably over the last few years thanks to the explosion in short-break holidays. It's a similar case with budget accommodation, where hip newcomers are proving that cheap can also mean chic.

Mary-Ann Gallagher

Romantic Hideaways

For a romantic getaway without breaking the bank, head for the Modernista mansion of **Hostal Palacios** *(see p159)*, while if you prefer rustic warmth, snuggle up in the wooden-beamed attic of **Hotel Sant Agustí** *(see p157)*. If expense isn't an issue, steal away to the chic **Neri H & R** *(see p155)*, a beautifully converted 18th-century palace.

Spas and Sports

Every imaginable luxury awaits at the **Gran Hotel La Florida** *(see p163)*, a hill-top retreat with spa, pool, gym and gardens. At the opulent **Casa Fuster** *(see p158)*, you can steam in the sauna and swim in the outdoor pool. The **Arts Barcelona** *(see p162)* lives up to its reputation as the city's most glamorous hotel with a spa, gym and panoramic pool.

Gastronomic Hotels

Many of Barcelona's hotels have excellent restaurants. **East 47** at the **Claris** *(see p158)* excels at fusion dishes, while super-stylish **Moo** at **Hotel Omm** *(see p161)*, serving contemporary Catalan cuisine, is the city's most talked-about hotel restaurant. For old-fashioned elegance and great service, nowhere beats **Caelis** at the **Hotel Palace** *(see p160)*.

choice stays

Style Statements

Slim, elegant **Hotel Park** *(see p156)* is an authentic 1950s gem and was one of the earliest Modernist style statements in the city. The fashionista favourite **Banys Orientals** *(see p155)* combines a stylish interior with a hip Born district address. The **Prestige Paseo de Gracia** *(see p160)* has a sleek minimalist interior and a classic 1930s façade.

Best of the Bargains

Hostal Jardí *(see p154)* is the city's most popular *hostal*, and enjoys a setting overlooking adjoining squares in the Barri Gòtic. For the hip traveller on a tight budget, the brightly painted **Gat Raval** *(see p156)* can't be beaten. The **Hotel Peninsular's** *(see p157)* rooms may be basic, but its plant-filled atrium is lovely and its central location a boon.

Views and Locales

The best rooms at the splendid **Hotel Colón** *(see p154)* boast balconies overlooking the Gothic cathedral and the street theatre of Plaça Nova. In the delightfully old-fashioned neighbourhood of Poblenou, **Hostal Poble Nou** *(see p163)* is handy for the beaches, while **Hotel Actual** *(see p159)* has a great location on the promenade of the Passeig de Gràcia.

Hotels

Hotel Colón *classic traditional hotel* `6 E2`
Avinguda de la Catedral 7 • 93 301 1404
» www.hotelcolon.es

Resolutely traditional, Hotel Colón is in a fabulous
location, opposite the dramatic spires of the
Cathedral. Its bedrooms are airy and decorated with
flowery prints, and those with views over Plaça Nova
are worth the extra expense. The hotel's plush terrace-
café also overlooks this lively square. **Moderate**

Hostal Fontanella *cosy home-from-home* `6 E1`
Vía Laietana 71, 2º • 93 317 5943
» www.hostalfontanella.com

A Modernista lift creaks up to the lobby, which is
crammed with dried flowers and knick-knacks. This
is a family-run *hostal*, and the friendly owners have
made the basic rooms rather cosy, with flowery
bedspreads and warm-hued paintwork. Street noise
can be a problem, so pack your ear plugs. **Cheap**

Hostal Jardí *prime location* `5 D3`
Plaça de Sant Josep Oriol 1 • 93 301 5900
» www.hoteljardi-barcelona.com

You'll need to book months in advance for a room in
Barcelona's most popular *hostal*, which is set in an
elegant, sgraffito-covered mansion bordering two
pretty squares and a church. The rooms are functional,
but impeccably clean – choose one with a balcony
overlooking one of the café-lined squares. **Cheap**

Hostal Rembrandt *simple budget hotel* `5 D2`
C/Portaferrissa 23, principal 1ª
» www.hostalrembrandt.com • 93 318 1011

This rickety *hostal* remains impervious to the whims
of fashion, and 1970s-style wicker furniture is much in
evidence. The rooms are spotless, however, and the
best of them have wrought-iron balconies overlooking
the buzzing shopping street. Seating areas dot the
corridors, and there's a breakfast room too. **Cheap**

Neri H & R *stylish hideaway* `5 D3`
C/Sant Sever 5 • 93 304 0655
» www.hotelneri.com

Hidden down a quiet alley in the heart of the Barri Gòtic, an 18th-century palace has been stunningly restored to house Barcelona's most enchanting hotel. The original stone staircase and wooden-beamed ceilings have been retained, but a wealth of contemporary art and sculpture brings it firmly up to date.

There are just 22 coolly stylish rooms, decorated with a mixture of antique and sleek contemporary furniture, and given a sensual touch by velvety rugs and beautiful fabrics in rich colours. All are equipped with gadgetry such as plasma TVs, and the designer bathrooms are supplied with scented toiletries.

Sip a cocktail on the Japanese-style roof terrace, which offers amazing views of the Cathedral, or browse art and design books on a velvet couch in the tranquil library. The **Neri Restaurant** is one of the most fashionable and romantic in the city. **Expensive**

Hotel Montecarlo *palace on the Ramblas* `5 C2`
Las Ramblas 124 • 93 412 0404
» www.montecarlobcn.com

The Montecarlo's lobby is incredibly sumptuous – a gorgeous whirl of gilt and marble. The hotel's generic rooms don't live up to the promise of the splendid entrance, but they are spacious, bright and well-equipped. Charming staff and an unbeatable location make this a great mid-budget choice. **Moderate**

Banys Orientals *affordable style* `6 F4`
C/Argenteria 37 • 93 268 8460
» www.hotelbanysorientals.com

Beloved by style magazines, this delightful boutique hotel is set in a handsome 19th-century mansion, with the city's best shopping and nightlife right on the doorstep. Rooms are small, but exquisitely decorated in pale, soothing colours and designer furnishings. The best for style on a budget. **Moderate**

» *Cheap: under €100 for a double room per night; moderate: €100–200; expensive: over €200*   **155**

Hotels

Hotel Park *1950s style icon* 6 G4

Avinguda Marquès de l'Argentera 11 • 93 319 6000
>> www.parkhotelbarcelona.com

Built between 1950 and 1953, this landmark hotel is a design classic. One of the city's earliest post-war Modernist buildings, it was constructed by prestigious Catalan architect Antoni Moragas, and handsomely restored by his son in 1990. The lobby bar is a gem, with its pairing of smooth chrome and a shimmering mosaic of white and turquoise tiles. However, it is the gorgeous wraparound staircase, spiralling sinuously, that provides the main highlight of the interior.

The rooms – which are smallish but extremely comfortable – have all been refurbished over the last few years in tasteful browns and creams. Best of the lot are the top floor rooms with balconies – they have fabulous views over the harbour.

Close to the chic boutiques and nightlife of the Born, the location is also handy for Barceloneta, the beaches and lovely Parc de la Ciutadella. **Moderate**

Gat Raval *hip budget hostal* 5 B1

C/Joaquín Costa 44 • 93 481 6670
>> www.gataccommodation.com

Easily the hippest budget hotel in Barcelona, Gat Raval is strikingly painted in a gleaming white and lime green colour scheme. Huge photographs of Barcelona give it a cool, urban feel, and it has quickly become one of the most popular *hostals* in the city, so early booking is essential. (Be warned, however – the online booking system is erratic, so it is best to confirm your reservation by phone.)

The 24 rooms are basic but immaculate, and all are decorated with crisp modern fabrics and furnishings; not all have en-suite bathrooms. However, all do have TVs, and there is free Internet access available to guests. The best rooms have views of MACBA *(see p83)*. The funky nightlife, galleries, restaurants and shopping of trendy Raval are on the doorstep, and the friendly staff are happy to give pointers to the neighbourhood's best attractions. **Cheap**

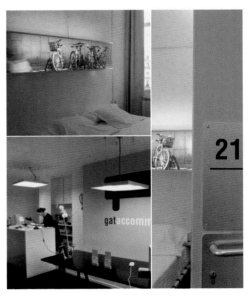

Hotel Peninsular *verdant former convent* `5 B3`
C/Sant Pau 34–6 • 93 302 3138
>> www.hpeninsular.com

A simple, peaceful retreat, the Peninsular was converted from a convent into an intimate little hotel back in 1870. It is perfectly set just a block away from the chaotic Ramblas, and is one of the best budget choices in the city. The building's central feature is a luminous atrium. Light pours in from a delicate skylight, and trailing plants spill through the stairwell. Tiled galleries fringe this space, with bedrooms leading off. The rooms are plain and functional – though presumably not quite as ascetic as they were when nuns lived here in the 19th century.

The antique furniture and fittings may have seen better days, but the walls are crisply painted in white and mint green, and everything is kept spotless. All rooms have en-suite bathrooms and air-conditioning – indispensable in the sultry summer heat. Breakfast is served in a high-ceilinged dining hall. **Cheap**

Hotel Sant Agustí *venerable old hotel* `5 C3`
Plaça de Sant Agustí 3 • 93 318 1658
>> www.hotelsa.com

Dating from 1840, this is the oldest hotel in the city. Its peach-painted façade fronts a handsome square that is dominated by an equally fine church. Despite the heritage of the building – it was a convent before becoming a hotel – the rooms are crisply modern, with smart, if slightly bland, decoration. Those in the attic have a touch of old-world charm thanks to exposed beams and sturdy wooden furniture. **Moderate**

Hotel Axel *top-notch gay hotel* `1 D5`
C/Aribau 33 • 93 323 9393
>> www.hotelaxel.com

Barcelona's best gay hotel, located close to the sights and shopping of Passeig de Gràcia. Many of the chic, contemporary rooms and suites have balconies, and the excellent amenities include a roof-top bar with fabulous views, a dipping pool, a boutique selling designer fashion, and a decent restaurant. **Moderate**

>> Hostals *are usually small, family-run hotels that won't necessarily have en-suite bathrooms or a lift*

Claris *fashionable art-filled hotel*   `2E4`
C/Pau Claris 150 • 93 487 6262
>> www.derbyhotels.es

Celebrities just love the Claris – a Modernista mansion with fabulous works of art adorning its walls. Rooms are luxuriously decorated with a mix of antique and contemporary furnishings, and there's a stunning roof-top pool and sun-deck. The hotel's East 47 restaurant serves excellent fusion cuisine. **Expensive**

Gallery Hotel *slick and contemporary*   `1 D4`
C/Rosselló 249 • 93 415 9911
>> www.galleryhotel.com

A smart, modern hotel, the Gallery offers spacious bedrooms, with striking black-and-white decor and state-of-the-art fittings. The fine restaurant overlooks a leafy garden, and guests can recover in the sauna from a hard day's sightseeing. Look for good weekend and summer deals on the website. **Expensive**

Casa Fuster *Modernista mansion*   `2 E3`
Passeig de Gràcia 132 • 93 255 3000
>> www.hotelcasafuster.com

Barcelona's newest luxury hotel is set in an opulent mansion designed by Lluís Domènech i Montaner *(see p89)*. Original sculptures and delicately curved wrought-iron balconies adorn the creamy façade, and arches and columns swirl with intricate floral motifs. The rooms and suites are sumptuously decorated, using plush fabrics and dark wooden furnishings that echo the style of the building. However, all rooms are equipped with the latest gadgetry, including flat screen TVs and Internet connections.

A panoramic terrace offers dazzling views along the grand sweep of the Passeig de Gràcia, while the hotel facilities include a fabulous outdoor swimming pool as well as a whirlpool and sauna. The lobby bar features enormous, velvety couches that echo the building's undulating lines, and Galaxó is one of Barcelona's best hotel restaurants. **Expensive**

Hostal Palacios *intimate gem*

2 E4

Rambla de Catalunya 27, 1º • 93 301 3079
>> www.hostalpalacios.com

This is perhaps the most delightful mid-price hotel in
the city, housed in a lavish Modernista building on
the tree-lined Rambla de Catalunya. There are just 11
rooms, all of which have retained many of the original
fittings, including beautiful tiled floors in glowing
colours, huge carved wooden doors (with massive
door keys to match), and swirling plasterwork.

Each bedroom is individually decorated, using
light, modern fabrics, and the bathrooms are all
modern in style, with opaque glass and chrome
fittings. Try to reserve one of the light-filled exterior
rooms if you can, particularly the larger, quieter
rooms at the back of the hotel. There is a comfortable
lounge area, with plush sofas and a small bar, and
visitors are welcome to play the piano. Guests also
have use of an Internet terminal, and other
amenities include a laundry service. **Cheap**

Hotel Actual *affordable and friendly*

1 D4

C/Rosselló 238 • 93 552 0550
>> www.hotelactual.com

Inexpensive places to stay are thin on the ground in
the chi-chi Eixample, which makes the Actual a good
hotel to know about. There's little in the way of
character, but rooms are elegantly minimalist, and the
sights and swanky boutiques of Passeig de Gràcia are
just around the corner. Great weekend rates. **Moderate**

Booking Agencies

The Barcelona tourist office offers an online booking
service at **www.barcelonaturisme.com**; alternatively,
call 93 285 3834. Many online booking agencies
frequently offer fantastic discounts. The most useful
and reliable include: **www.barcelona-on-line.es**
(which has a good section on last-minute deals);
www.alpharooms.com; **www.expedia.co.uk**; and

www.freehotelsearch.com. Budget travellers should
try booking through **www.travellerspoint.com**, or
www.eurocheapo.com.

For accommodation elsewhere in Catalunya,
contact the Catalan tourist information office
(**www.gencat.es**) in the Palau Robert, Passeig de
Gràcia 107. They can also be contacted by calling
90 240 0012 (just dial 012 from within Catalunya).

>> *Besides the online booking agencies listed above, hotel websites also regularly post special deals*

Prestige Paseo de Gracia *deluxe*   `2 E5`

Passeig de Gràcia 62 • 93 272 4180
>> www.prestigepaseodegracia.com

This sleek, minimalist hotel is tucked behind a classic 1930s façade on the vibrant Passeig de Gràcia. The light, tranquil rooms are sparely decorated in cool colours, but the fabrics are thick and sensuous. All rooms have up-to-the-minute amenities, including Bang & Olufsen TVs and music systems – some even boast sun-decks and loungers. The stylish bathrooms are loaded with Etro toiletries.

The hotel is small, with just 45 rooms, which gives it an intimate and personal feel, and the "Ask Me" service ensures that a team of employees is always on hand for any query or request. Passeig de Gràcia is fantastic for shopping, and should you need your purchases carried back to your room, the hotel will send someone to collect them. Breakfast and snacks are served in the Zeroom, where you can also linger over a collection of art and design books. **Expensive**

Hotel Palace *opulent luxury hotel*   `2 F5`

Gran Via de les Corts Catalanes 668 • 93 510 1130
>> www.hotelpalacebarcelona.com

The Grande Dame of Barcelona's hotel scene, this hotel (formerly the Ritz) first opened its doors in 1919, and the roll call of famous guests has included everyone from Spanish royals to Salvador Dalí. Its wedding-cake exterior oozes exuberant plaster decoration like icing, while doormen in top hats and tails usher guests into a resplendent lobby, filled with polished marble and glittering chandeliers.

The bedrooms are deeply traditional, with elegant drapes, burnished antiques and plush fabrics. Some have large marble bathrooms, with mosaic tiling and gilded fittings seemingly inspired by the spas of ancient Rome. For formal dining, there's the elegant Caelis, and for a pre- or post-meal drink, the Scotch Bar – sink into a leather armchair while expert bar staff prepare your drink. In summer, breakfast is served in the pretty garden. **Expensive**

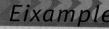

Hotel Omm *über-cool hotel* `1 D4`
C/Rosselló 265 • 93 445 4000
>> www.hotelomm.es

Barcelona's most extraordinary new hotel is housed in a highly original building in the Eixample, designed by award-winning Catalan architect Juli Capella. Curving balconies appear to peel out from the smooth façade, and the standard, box-like public areas of traditional hotels have been replaced with a luminous, amorphous space that contains the reception, lobby and destination restaurant Moo *(see p42)*. This elegant restaurant is one of the most popular in the city, and the adjoining bar, with its chic sofas and contemporary fireplace, is always packed with a beautiful crowd.

In deliberate contrast to the dark corridors, the rooms are bright and light, with blond parquet floors, crisp modern fabrics and stunning contemporary bathrooms. You can relax in the brand new spa, or up on the roof-deck, where elegant white loungers are laid out for sunbathing; there's also a small pool. Best of all, however, are the magnificent views from the deck, which take in the twisting rooftop chimneys on Gaudí's La Pedrera *(see p76)*. **Expensive**

Hotels

Arts Barcelona *beachfront glamour* `7 A4`
C/Marina 19–21 • 93 221 1000
>> www.hotelartsbarcelona.com

Located in a spectacular tower of exposed steel and glass overlooking Port Olímpic, the Hotel Arts is the last word in contemporary luxury. The top 10 floors (there are 44 in all) contain ultra-luxurious apartments with butler service, but all the hotel's immense rooms and fabulous suites offer stunning, elegant decor and magnificent sea views. They have every conceivable amenity, from vast, stylish bathrooms to the latest TVs and CD players.

Specially commissioned works by Spanish artists adorn the luminous interior, while the extensive list of amenities includes an outdoor swimming pool and hot plunge pool surrounded by palm-filled gardens. There is also a gym with steam room and sauna, a brand new spa with magnificent ocean views, and a fabulous restaurant. To top it all off, the hotel is only steps from the beach. **Expensive**

Sea Point Hostel *beachside bargain* `4 G5`
Plaça del Mar 1–4 • 93 224 7075
>> www.seapointhostel.com

This budget backpacker's hostel is right on the seafront: step out the front door and you are literally on the beach. It offers dorm accommodation for 4–8 people, and each room has its own bathroom. Free Internet access is available, bike hire can be arranged and breakfast is included in the price. **Cheap**

Short-Stay Apartment Agencies

There are many agencies in Barcelona that specialize in short-term property rental. One of the best is **www.oh-barcelona.com** (087 147 400 95 from the UK). It has a wide range of apartments in all price brackets, and provides an efficient, friendly service. The website **www.rentals-barcelona.com** focuses on properties mainly in the moderate and inexpensive category. **www.barcelonaforrent.com** (93 458 6340) offers well-equipped apartments that are geared towards business travellers as well as tourists. Barcelona also has several aparthotels, which combine the convenience of a private apartment with the services of a hotel. Citadines Aparthotels (**www.citadines.com**; 93 270 1111) are centrally situated on the Ramblas (No. 122).

Hotel H10 Marina *well-located hotel* `7 B3`

Avinguda Bogatell 64–8 • 93 309 7917
>> www.h10.es

This hotel is part of a reliable chain and, while it does not ooze charm, it is in a great location – near the beaches and Port Olímpic, and close to good transport links for the city centre. The spacious rooms are tastefully decorated and bright, and the hotel's excellent amenities include pools and a spa. **Expensive**

Hostal Poble Nou *charming guesthouse* `7 D3`

C/Taulat 30 • 93 221 2601
>> www.hostalpoblenou.com

This pastel-painted townhouse dates from the 1930s, and the handful of pretty guest rooms have kept some of the original details. It's in the delightful, old-fashioned neighbourhood of Poblenou, a 10-minute metro or tram ride from the city centre, and just a stone's throw from the best city beaches. **Cheap**

Gran Hotel La Florida *hilltop mansion*

C/Vallvidrera al Tibidabo 83–93 • 93 259 3000
>> www.hotellaflorida.com

Breathtakingly set in the Collserola hills overlooking Barcelona, this magnificent hotel is an oasis of calm and beauty. The creamy mansion is surrounded by luxuriant gardens, and many of the gorgeous rooms and suites have been designed by celebrated artists and interior designers. All are decorated in pale, soothing colours, and many boast Jacuzzis, private gardens and stunning views across the city below.

Amenities include a luxurious spa with an indoor-outdoor stainless steel pool which appears to spill over the side of the mountain, a gym, an elegant formal restaurant, L'Orangerie, a bar and a nightclub with regular live jazz. The natural park of the Collserola is on the doorstep, and can be explored by bicycle or on horseback. If you can tear yourself away from the hotel, a limousine is available to drop you off in the heart of the city. **Expensive**

The heart of Barcelona is the Old City (Ciutat Vella), comprising the Barri Gòtic, Raval and Born neighbourhoods. To the north of the Old City is the formally planned Eixample district, where most of the city's Modernista buildings are situated. To the southeast of the Old City is densely populated Barceloneta and the wealthier area of Port Olímpic. Almost every listing in this guide features a (boxed) page and grid reference to the maps in this section. Entries that fall outside the mapped area give transport details instead.

Key to Street Finder

- ▦ Sight/public building
- Ⓜ Metro station
- Ⓡ RENFE station
- Ⓖ FGC station
- ⓑ Bus station
- ⊖ River boat pier
- Ⓒ Coach station
- ⊞ Tram terminus
- ⊜ Funicular terminus
- ⓘ Tourist information office
- ⊜ Taxi rank
- Ⓟ Police station
- ✚ Hospital with casualty unit
- ✛ Church
- ⊗ Post office
- Ⓟ Car park
- ▬ Pedestrian street
- ══ Railway line
- ●━● Funicular railway

Scale of maps 1–4 and 7

0 metres	400
0 yards	400

Scale of maps 5–6

0 metres	200
0 yards	200

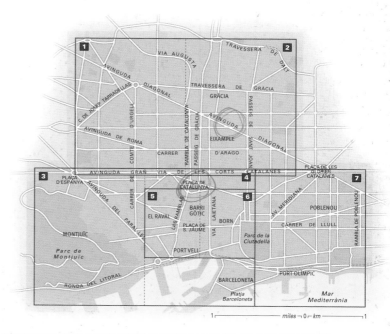

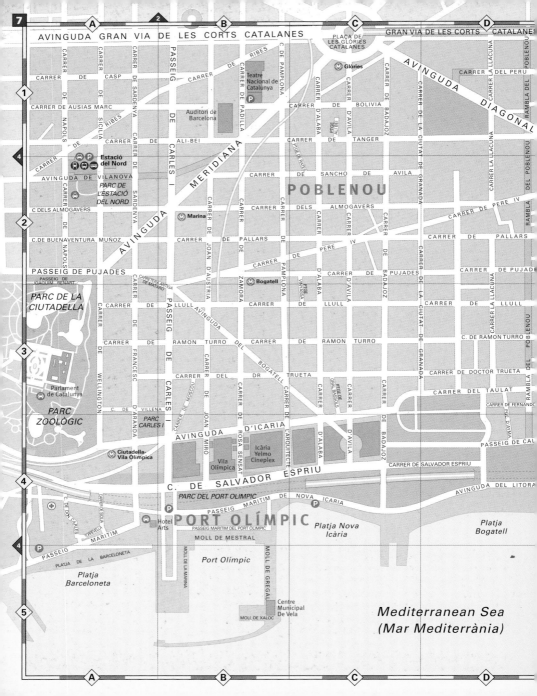

Street Finder Index

Sombreria Obach (p53)
Hats

Women's Secret (p57)
Lingerie

Xocoa (p55)
Chocolates

Zara (p60)
Fashion chain

Born

Alea (p61)
Jewellery

Almacen Marabi (p63)
Toyshop

Arlequi Mascares (p57)
Carnival masks

Bijou Brigitte (p61)
Jewellery

BoccaBacco (p63)
Delicatessen

La Botifarreria de
Santa Maria (p62)
Delicatessen

Cafes El Magnifico (p61)
Coffee roaster

Carrer Sant Pere
mes Baix (p132)
Shopping street

Casa Gispert (p62)
Delicatessen

Como Agua de Mayo (p61)
Fashion

Custo (p62)
Fashion

Czar (pp62 & 132)
Shoes

Desigual (p57)
Fashion

Farmacia Fonoll (p132)
Pharmacy

Fior di Loto (p63)
Shoes

Iguapop (p64)
Art

Kwatra (p64)
Sportswear

Ona Joia (p61)
Jewellery

Opera Prima (p61)
Jewellery

Passeig del Born (p132)
Shopping street

Recdi8 (p62)
Designer homewares

La Sabateria
del Born (p61)
Shoes

Sans & Sans (p61)
Tea and tea sets

Santa Caterina
Market (p132)
Market

Vila Viniteca (p64)
Wine and spirits

Raval

Arantxa (p65)
Delicatessen

Camper (p67)
Shoes

CD Drome (p64)
Records

Cinemascope (p66)
Cinema memorabilia

Discos Castello (p65)
Records

Discos Edison's (p65)
Records

Estanc Mesequino (p65)
Cigars and pipes

Giménez y Zuazo (p64)
Fashion

Holala (p65)
Vintage clothes

Lailo (p65)
Vintage clothes

Mercat de Sant Antoni (p66)
Market

Smart And Clean (p65)
Vintage clothes

Torres (p66)
Wine

Art & Architecture

Barri Gòtic

Capella de Santa
Àgata (p78)
Historic building

Catedral de
Barcelona (pp12 & 79)
Religious building

Centre d'Art Santa
Mònica (p131)
Art centre

Museu del Calçot (p142)
Museum

Museu Frederic
Marès (p79)
Museum

Museu d'Història
de la Ciutat (pp78 & 130)
*Museum & historic
buildings*

Palau Reial (p130)
Historic building

Roman Ruins of
Barcino (pp78 & 130)
Historic buildings

Saló del Tinell (p78)
Historic building

Shlomo Ben Adret
Synagogue (p79)
Religious building

Born

Basílica de Santa María
del Mar (p82)
Religious building

Maeght Gallery (p80)
Gallery

Metrònom (p85)
Gallery

Museu Picasso (p81)
Museum

Museu Tèxtil i
d'Indumentària (p80)
Fashion museum

Museu de la
Xocolata (p82)
Chocolate museum

Raval

Barcelona Institute
of Culture (p80)
Exhibition space

CCCB (p82)
Exhibition space

Esglesia de Sant Pau
del Camp (pp84 & 144)
Religious building

MACBA (Museu d'Art
Contemporani de
Barcelona) (p83)
Museum

Museu Marítim (p84)
Museum

Palau Güell (p76)
Historic building

Palau de la
Virreina (p80)
Exhibition space

La Santa (p80)
Gallery

Performance

Barri Gòtic

Gran Teatre del
Liceu (p96)
Opera house

Harlem Jazz Club (p97)
Jazz venue

Teatre Poliorama (p97)
Theatre

Born

L'Hivernacle de la
Ciutadella (pp97 & 115)
Jazz venue

Palau de la Música
Catalana (pp15 & 98)
Classical concert hall

Parc de la Ciutadella
(classical concerts
& swing) (p97)
Music & dance

Raval

El Cangrejo (p99)
Cabaret

Index by Area

Old City

Bars & Clubs

Barri Gòtic

Bar La Plata (p110)
Wine bar

Boadas (p110)
Cocktail bar

Bosc de les Fades (p110)
Café-bar

Café Royale (p110)
Lounge bar

Club 13 (p112)
Club & restaurant

Las Cuevas del Sorte (p113)
Café-bar

Dot (p111)
Club

Fonfone (p111)
DJ bar

Ginger (p111)
Cocktail & tapas bar

Jamboree (p113)
Music bar

Júpiter (p113)
Bar

La Palma (p112)
Bodega bar

Pilé 43 (p112)
Cocktail bar

Pipa Club (p112)
Bar

Salvation (p122)
Club

Born

Borneo (p114)
Bar

Flow (p114)
Cocktail bar

Fluxia (p114)
DJ bar

Gimlet (p114)
Cocktail bar

L'Hivernacle de la Ciutadella (pp115 & 143)
Café-bar

Pitín Bar (p115)
Café-bar

Plàstic Café (p115)
DJ bar/club

República (p116)
Club

Va de Ví (p117)
Tapas bar

El Xampanyet (p117)
Tapas bar

Raval

Ambar (pp117 & 134)
DJ bar

Aurora (p116)
Bar

Bar Pastís (p116)
Bar

Benidorm (p117)
Bar/club

El Café Que Pone Muebles Navarro (p116)
Cocktail bar

La Concha (p118)
Bar

La Confitería (p117)
Café-bar

Jazz Sí Club (p118)
Music bar

Madame Jasmine (p118)
Bar

Mam i Teca (p117)
Tapas bar

Marsella (p118)
Bar

Metro (p119)
Club

La Paloma (p118)
Club

Quimet & Quimet (p117)
Tapas bar

Zelig (p119)
Music bar

Zentraus Dance Club (p119)
Club

Streetlife

Barri Gòtic

L'Antiquari de la Plaça del Rei (p130)
Café

Arts & Crafts Market (p131)
Market

Boqueria (p131)
Market

Café de l'Òpera (p131)
Café

Centre d'Art Santa Mònica (p131)
Art centre

Museu d'Història de la Ciutat (pp78 & 130)
Museum

Palau Reial (p130)
Historic building

Plaça del Rei (p130)
City square

Las Ramblas (pp13 & 131)
Shopping street & markets

Roman Ruins of Barcino (pp78 & 130)

Born

Carrer Sant Pere mes Baix (p132)
Shopping street

Farmacia Fonoll (p132)
Pharmacy

Passeig del Born (p132)
Shopping street

Santa Caterina Market (p132)
Market

Santa María del Mar (p132)
Religious building

Raval

Ambar (pp117 & 134)
Café-bar

Café de les Delicies (p134)
Café

Kasparo (pp36 & 135)
Café-bar

Oolong (p135)
Café

Plaça Vicenç Martorell (p135)
City square

Rambla del Raval (p134)
City street

Havens

Barri Gòtic

Café de l'Acadèmia (pp29 & 142)
Café-restaurant

Museu del Calçot (p142)
Museum

Plaça de Sant Felìp Neri (p142)
City square

Plaça Sants Just i Pastor (p142)
City square

Salterio (p144)
Tea room

Born

L'Hivernacle de la Ciutadella (pp115 & 143)
Café

Parc de la Ciutadella (p143)
Park

Raval

Església de Sant Pau del Camp (pp84 & 144)
Religious building

Hotels

Barri Gòtic

Hostal Fontanella (p154)
Cheap

Hostal Jardí (p154)
Cheap

Hostal Rembrandt (p154)
Cheap

Hotel Colón (p154)
Moderate

Hotel Montecarlo (p155)
Moderate

Neri H & R (p155)
Moderate

Born

Banys Orientals (p155)
Moderate

Hotel Park (p156)
Moderate

Raval

Gat Raval (p156)
Cheap

Hotel Peninsular (p157)
Cheap

Hotel Sant Agustí (p157)
Moderate

Barceloneta

Restaurants

Can Solé (p35) €€
Seafood

Daguiri (pp36 & 123) €
Café

Set Portes (p35) €€
Paella

Bars & Clubs

Can Ganassa (p123 & 133)
Bar

Can Ramonet (p123)
Bar

CDLC (p123)
Club, bar & restaurant

Daguiri (pp36 & 123)
Bar

Sal Café (p124)
Café-bar

El Vaso de Oro (p123)
Bar

Streetlife

Barceloneta Market (p133)
Market

Can Ganassa
(pp123 & 133)
Tapas bar

Havens

Club Natació Atlètic
Barceloneta (p145)
Fitness centre

Platja de Barceloneta (p144)
Beach

Platja de Sant Sebastià (p144)
Beach

Hotels

Sea Point Hostel (p162)
Cheap

Port Olímpic

Restaurants

A La Menta (p37) €€
Paella

Agua (p36) €€
Mediterranean

Arola (p36) €€€
Tapas

Bestial (p37) €€
Italian

Xiringuito Escribà (p37) €€
Seafood

Havens

Platja de Bogatell (p144)
Beach

Platja Mar Bella (p144)
Beach

Platja de Nova Icària (p144)
Beach

Hotels

Arts Barcelona (p162)
Expensive

Hotel H10 Marina (p163)
Moderate

Poblenou

Performance

Razzmatazz (p104)
Rock & pop venue

Bars & Clubs

Oven (p127)
Lounge bar & restaurant

Streetlife

El Tio Che (p132)
Café

Rambla del Poblenou (p132)
City street

Hotels

Hostal Poble Nou (p163)
Cheap

Montjuïc

Restaurants

El Font del Gat (p145) €€
Park restaurant

Art & Architecture

CaixaForum (p85)
Exhibition space

Fundació
Joan Miró (p87)
Museum

MNAC (Museu Nacional
d'Art de Catalunya (p86)
Museum

Pavelló Mies van
der Rohe (p85)
Historic building

Performance

Estadi Olímpic
(RCD Espanyol) (p101)
Football stadium

Mercat de les
Flors (p100)
Theatre

Palau Sant Jordi (p99)
Rock venue

El Tablao de
Carmen (p100)
Flamenco venue

Teatre Grec (p100)
Theatre

Teatre Lliure (p99)
Theatre

Tinta Roja (p101)
Tango venue

Bars & Clubs

Barcelona Rouge (p122)
Cocktail bar

Discothèque (p123)
Club

Sala Apolo (p122)
Club

Havens

El Font del Gat (p145)
Park restaurant

Jardins de Laribal (p145)
Park

Joan Miró Sculpture
Park (p145)
Park

Eixample

Restaurants

Alkimia (p37) €€€
Fusion

Casa Calvet (p38) €€€
Catalan

Cinc Sentits (p39) €€€
Fusion

El Japonés (p38) €€
Sushi

Moo (p42) €€€
Modern Mediterranean

Noti (p40) €€€
Mediterranean

Principal (p41) €€€
Mediterranean

Le Relais de €€
Venise (p38)
French

Semproniana (p38) €€
Catalan

Shibui (p41) €€€
Japanese

Sol de Nit (p126)
Bar

Sol Soler (p136)
Bar-café

Streetlife

Café del Sol (pp125 & 136)
Bar-café

Mercat de la Llibertat (p136)
Market

Mond Bar (p126 & 136)
DJ bar

Plaça del Sol (p136)
City square

Sol de Nit (p126 & 136)
Bar

Sol Soler (p136)
Bar-café

Havens

Plaça Virreina (p146)
City square

Pedralbes & Les Corts

Art & Architecture

Monestir de Pedralbes (p90)
Historic building

Museu de les Arts Decoratives (p90)
Museum

Museu de Ceràmica (p90)
Museum

Palau Reial de Pedralbes (p90)
Historic buildings & museum

Performance

Bikini (p104)
Rock & pop venue

Nou Camp (FC Barcelona) (p105)
Football stadium

Palau Blaugrana (p104)
Basketball stadium

Bars & Clubs

Elephant (p126)
Lounge bar & club

Havens

Iradier (p146)
Spa & treatments

Horta

Restaurants

Can Travi Nou (p45)
Catalan

Havens

Jardins de Laberint d'Horta (p146)
Gardens

Tibidabo

Bars & Clubs

Danzatoria (p127)
Club & restaurant

Mirablau (p127)
Café-bar

Havens

Monastery of Sant Cugat (p147)
Religious building

Parc Natural de Collserola (p147)
Park

Hotels

Gran Hotel La Florida (p163)
Expensive

Beyond the City

Restaurants

Garraf

Gaudí-Garraf (p148)
Castle restaurant

Girona

Celler de Can Roca (p46) €€€
Experimental Catalan

Sant Celoni

Racó de Can Fabes (p45) €€€
Catalan

Sant Pol

Sant Pau (p46) €€€
Catalan

Roses

El Bulli (p47) €€€
Cutting-edge cuisine

Sitges

Montroig Café (p139) €
Café-bar

La Santa María (p139) €€
Traditional restaurant

El Velero (p139) €€€
Seafood restaurant

Vic

Cardona 7 (p45) €€
Experimental tapas

Art & Architecture

Figueres

Teatre-Museu Dalí (p90)
Museum

Girona

Banys Àrabs (p91)
Historic building

Girona Cathedral (p91)
Religious building & museum

Montserrat

Monastery (p148)
Religious building

Sitges

Cau Ferrat (p138)
Historic building & museum

Museu Maricel de Mar (p138)
Museum

Tarragona

Museu d'Història de Tarragona (p149)
Museum

Museu Nacional Arqueològic (p149)
Museum

Old City (p149)
Historical buildings

Streetlife

Sitges

Extreme (p139)
Fashion boutique

Montroig Café (p139)
Café-bar

Oscar (p139)
Swimwear

Pachito (p139)
Music bar

Parrot Pub (p139)
Bar

La Santa María (p139) €€
Restaurant

El Velero (p139) €€€
Restaurant

Vic

Plaça Major (p137)
City square & market

Havens

Garraf

Garraf Beach (p148)
Beach

Gaudí-Garraf (p148) €€€
Restaurant

Montserrat

Monastery and Natural Park (p148)
Religious building & park

Tarragona

Museu d'Història de Tarragona (p149)
Museum

Museu Nacional Arqueològic (p149)
Museum

Old City (p149)
Historical buildings

Restaurants

Asian

Mosquito (p31) €
Old City/Born

Basque

Laurak (p44) €€
Gràcia

Cafés

Arc Café (p28) €
Old City/Barri Gòtic

Café d'Estiu (p36) €
Old City/Barri Gòtic

Café La Granja (p55) €
Old City/Barri Gòtic

Daguiri (pp36 & 123) €
Barceloneta

Dos Trece (p44) €
Old City/Raval

Escribà (p44) €
Old City/Barri Gòtic

La Fianna (p44) €
Old City/Born

Kasparo (pp36 & 135) €
Old City/Raval

Ra (p34) €
Old City/Raval

Schilling (p28) €
Old City/Barri Gòtic

Tèxtil Café (p36) €
Old City/Born

Catalan

El Bulli (p47) €€€
Beyond the City/Roses

Café de l'Acadèmia (p29) €€
Old City/Barri Gòtic

Can Culleretes (p28) €
Old City/Barri Gòtic

Can Travi Nou (p45) €€€
Horta

Casa Calvet (p38) €€€
Eixample

Celler de Can Roca (p46) €€€
Beyond the City/Girona

El Convent (p34) €
Old City/Raval

Pitarra (p29) €€
Old City/Barri Gòtic

Els Quatre Gats (p30) €€
Old City/Barri Gòtic

Racó de Can Fabes (p45) €€€
Beyond the City/Sant Celoni

La Santa María (p139) €€
Beyond the City/Sitges

Sant Pau (p46) €€€
Beyond the City/Sant Pol

Semproniana (p38) €€
Eixample

Cuban

Habana Vieja (p33) €€
Old City/Born

Desserts

Espai Sucre (p31) €€€
Old City/Born

French

Abac (p31) €€€
Old City/Born

L'Ou Com Balla (p33) €€
Old City/Born

Le Relais de Venise (p38) €€
Eixample

Fusion

Alkimia (p37) €€€
Eixample

Cinc Sentits (p39) €€€
Eixample

Greek

Dionisos (p30) €
Old City/Born

Indian

Govinda (p28) €
Old City/Barri Gòtic

Italian

Bestial (p37) €€
Port Olímpic

Gente de Pasta (p33) €€
Old City/Born

Japanese

El Japonés (p38) €€
Eixample

Shibui (p41) €€€
Eixample

Mediterranean

Abac (p31) €€€
Old City/Born

Agua (p36) €€
Port Olímpic

Biblioteca (p35) €€
Old City/Raval

És (p34) €€
Old City/Raval

Little Italy (p33) €€
Old City/Born

Moo (p42) €€€
Eixample

Noti (p40) €€€
Eixample

Ot (p43) €€€
Gràcia

Principal (p41) €€€
Eixample

Les Quinze Nits (p28) €
Old City/Barri Gòtic

El Salón (p29) €€
Old City/Barri Gòtic

Mexican

Chido One (p43) €
Gràcia

Dos Trece (p44) €
Old City/Raval

Moroccan

L'Ou Com Balla (p33) €€
Old City/Born

Paella

A La Menta (p37) €€
Port Olímpic

Set Portes (p35) €€
Barceloneta

Seafood

Botafumeiro (p44) €€€
Gràcia

Cal Pep (p32) €€
Old City/Born

Can Solé (p35) €€
Barceloneta

Casa Leopoldo (p35) €€
Old City/Raval

La Paradeta (p32) €€
Old City/Born

El Velero (p139) €€€
Beyond the City/Sitges

Xiringuito Escribà (p37) €€
Port Olímpic

Spanish

Los Caracoles (p29) €€
Old City/Barri Gòtic

Sushi

El Japonés (p38) €€
Eixample

Tapas

Arola (p36) €€€
Port Olímpic

Cal Pep (p32) €€
Old City/Born

Cardona 7 (p45) €€
Beyond the City/Vic

Comerç 24 (p32) €€€
Old City/Born

Taller de Tapas (p30) €€
Old City/Barri Gòtic

Tortillas

Flash Flash (p43) €
Gràcia

Vegetarian

Govinda (p28)
Old City/Barri Gòtic   €

L'Illa de Gràcia (p43)
Gràcia   €

Sésamo (p34)
Old City/Raval   €

Shopping

Accessories

Alonso (p56)
Old City/Barri Gòtic

Rafa (p60)
Old City/Barri Gòtic

Antiques & Artifacts

Bulevard dels Antiquaris (p69)
Eixample

Ciutad (p60)
Old City/Barri Gòtic

Cronos (p69)
Eixample

La Gauche Divine (p54)
Old City/Barri Gòtic

Iguapop (p64)
Old City/Born

Raquel Montagut (p69)
Eixample

Tric Trac (p69)
Eixample

Art Prints

March (p69)
Eixample

Bookshops

Altaïr (p66)
Eixample

La Central (p70)
Eixample

Dom (p53)
Old City/Barri Gòtic

Children's Clothes

Els Angels (p57)
Old City/Barri Gòtic

Cigars & Pipes

Estanc Mesequino (p65)
Old City/Raval

Confectionery

Cacao Sampaka (p68)
Eixample

Humm (p70)
Eixample

Papabubble (p53)
Old City/Barri Gòtic

Planelles Donat (p60)
Old City/Barri Gòtic

Xocoa (p55)
Old City/Barri Gòtic

Cosmetics

Herboristeria del Rei (p54)
Old City/Barri Gòtic

Department Stores, Superstores & Malls

El Corte Inglés (p68)
Eixample

FNAC (p67)
Eixample

Galerias Malda (p57)
Old City/Barri Gòtic

Vinçon (p71)
Eixample

Fashion

Angel Gimeno (p53)
Old City/Barri Gòtic

Aragaza (p57)
Old City/Barri Gòtic

Camisería Pons (p71)
Gràcia

Como Agua de Mayo (p61)
Old City/Born

Contribuciones y Moda (p71)
Gràcia

Custo (p62)
Old City/Born

Desigual (p57)
Old City/Born

La Gauche Divine (p54)
Old City/Barri Gòtic

Giménez y Zuazo (p64)
Old City/Raval

Loft Avignon (p53)
Old City/Barri Gòtic

Mango (pp57 & 60)
Old City/Barri Gòtic

Produit National Brut (p53)
Old City/Barri Gòtic

Purificación García (p68)
Eixample

So_da (p53)
Old City/Barri Gòtic

Zara (p60)
Old City/Barri Gòtic

Food & Drink

Arantxa (p65)
Old City/Raval

BoccaBacco (p63)
Old City/Born

La Botifarreria de Santa Maria (p62)
Old City/Born

Caelum (p54)
Old City/Barri Gòtic

Cafes El Magnifico (p61)
Old City/Born

Casa Gispert (p62)
Old City/Born

Colmado Quilez (p69)
Eixample

Formatgeria La Seu (p52)
Old City/Barri Gòtic

Mantequeria Ravell (p70)
Eixample

Sans & Sans (p61)
Old City/Born

Torres (p66)
Old City/Raval

Vila Viniteca (p64)
Old City/Born

Furniture

Gemma Povo (p55)
Old City/Barri Gòtic

Germanes Garcia (p55)
Old City/Barri Gòtic

Gifts

Items d'Ho (p70)
Eixample

Hats

Sombreria Obach (p53)
Old City/Barri Gòtic

Homewares

Caixa de Fang (p52)
Old City/Barri Gòtic

Kaveh Abadani (p63)
Old City/Born

Lisboa (p70)
Eixample

Recdi8 (p62)
Old City/Born

Jewellery

Alea (p61)
Old City/Born

Bagués (p69)
Eixample

Bijou Brigitte (p61)
Old City/Born

Elisa Brunells (p63)
Old City/Born

Hipotesi (p71)
Eixample

Kaveh Abadani (p63)
Old City/Born

Ona Joia (p61)
Old City/Born

Opera Prima (p61)
Old City/Born

Platamundi (p57)
Old City/Barri Gòtic

El Taller (p70)
Eixample

Roman Ruins of
Barcino (pp78 & 130)
Old City/Barri Gòtic

Saló del Tinell (p78)
Old City/Barri Gòtic

Tarragona Old City (p149)
Beyond the City/Tarragona

Museums

Cau Ferrat (p138)
Beyond the City/Sitges

**Centre d'Art
Santa Mònica** (p131)
Old City/Barri Gòtic

Fundació Antoni Tàpies (p88)
Eixample

Fundació Joan Miró (pp14 & 87)
Montjuïc

**Fundación Francisco
Godia** (p88)
Eixample

**MACBA (Museu d'Art Contem-
porani de Barcelona)** (p83)
Old City/Raval

**MNAC (Museu Nacional d'Art
de Catalunya)** (pp14 & 86)
Montjuïc

**Museu de les Arts
Decoratives** (p90)
Pedralbes & Les Corts

Museu del Calçat (p142)
Old City/Barri Gòtic

Museu de Ceràmica (p90)
Pedralbes & Les Corts

**Museu Egipci
de Barcelona** (p88)
Eixample

Museu Frederic Marès (p79)
Old City/Barri Gòtic

**Museu d'Història
de la Ciutat** (pp78 & 130)
Old City/Barri Gòtic

**Museu d'Història de
Tarragona** (p149)
Beyond the City/Tarragona

Museu Maricel de Mar (p138)
Beyond the City/Sitges

Museu Marítim (p84)
Old City/Raval

**Museu Nacional
Arqueològic** (p149)
Beyond the City/Tarragona

Museu Picasso (pp14 & 81)
Old City/Born

**Museu Tèxtil i
d'Indumentària** (p80)
Old City/Born

Museu de la Xocolata (p82)
Old City/Born

**Palau Reial de
Pedralbes** (p90)
Pedralbes & Les Corts

Teatre Museu Dalí (p90)
Beyond the City/Figueres

Religious Buildings

**Basílica de Santa María
del Mar** (p82)
Old City/Born

Catedral de Barcelona
(pp12 & 79)
Old City/Barri Gòtic

**Esglesia de Sant Pau
del Camp** (pp84 & 144)
Old City/Raval

Girona Cathedral (p91)
Beyond the City/Girona

**Monestir de
Pedralbes** (p90)
Pedralbes & Les Corts

Montserrat Monastery (p148)
*Beyond the City/
Montserra*

Sagrada Família (pp12 & 76)
Eixample

**Shlomo Ben Adret
Synagogue** (p79)
Old City/Barri Gòtic

Performance

Classical Venues

L'Auditori de Barcelona (p103)
Eixample

**Palau de la Música
Catalana** (pp15, 89 & 98)
Old City/Born

Parc de la Ciutadella (p97)
Old City/Born

Cinemas

Coliseum (p103)
Eixample

**FilmoTeca de la Generalitat
de Catalunya** (p102)
Eixample

Méliès (p102)
Eixample

Renoir Floridablanca (p103)
Eixample

Dance & Cabaret

El Cangrejo (p99)
Old City/Raval

Luz de Gas (p103)
Eixample

**El Tablao de
Carmen** (p100)
Montjuïc

Tinta Roja (p101)
Montjuïc

Jazz

Harlem Jazz Club (p97)
Old City/Barri Gòtic

**L'Hivernacle de la
Ciutadella** (pp97, 115 & 143)
Old City/Born

**Parc de la
Ciutadella** (p97)
Old City/Born

**La Pedrera
(rooftop jazz)** (p103)
Eixample

Pop & Rock Venues

Bikini (p104)
Pedralbes & Les Corts

Palau Sant Jordi (p99)
Montjuïc

Razzmatazz (p104)
Poblenou

Sports Arenas

**Estadi Olímpic
(RCD Espanyol)** (p101)
Montjuïc

**Nou Camp
(FC Barcelona)** (p105)
*Pedralbes &
Les Corts*

Palau Blaugrana (p104)
*Pedralbes &
Les Corts*

Theatres

Gran Teatre del Liceu (p96)
Old City/Barri Gòtic

Mercat de les Flors (p100)
Montjuïc

Teatre Grec (p100)
Montjuïc

Teatre Lliure (p99)
Montjuïc

**Teatre Nacional
de Catalunya** (p102)
Eixample

Teatre Poliorama (p97)
Old City/Barri Gòtic

Bars & Clubs

Bars

Aurora (p116)
Old City/Raval

Bar Pastís (p116)
Old City/Raval

Benidorm (p117)
Old City/Raval

Borneo (p114)
Old City/Born

Can Ganassa (p123 & 133)
Barceloneta

Can Ramonet (p123)
Barceloneta

La Concha (p118)
Old City/Raval

Daguiri (p123)
Barceloneta

General Index

Acknowledgments

Produced by Blue Island Publishing
www.blueisland.co.uk
Editorial Director Rosalyn Thiro
Art Director Stephen Bere
Commissioning Editor Michael Ellis
Fact Checker Alix Leveugle
Proofreader Val Phoenix
Picture Researcher Amaia Allende

Published by DK
Publishing Managers Jane Ewart and Scarlett O'Hara
Senior Editor Christine Stroyan
Senior Designers Paul Jackson and Marisa Renzullo
Website Editor Gouri Banerji
Cartographic Editor Casper Morris
Senior Cartographer Uma Bhattacharya
DTP Designers Jason Little and Natasha Lu
Production Coordinator Louise Minihane
Fact Checker Paula Canal

PHOTOGRAPHY PERMISSIONS

The publishers would like to thank all the churches, museums, hotels, restaurants, bars, clubs, shops, galleries and other sights for their assistance and kind permission to photograph at their establishments.

Placement Key: tl = top left; tr = top right; c = centre; cl = centre left; cla = centre left above; clb = centre left below; cr = centre right; crb = centre right below; b = bottom; bl = bottom left; br = bottom right.; tc = top centre.

The publishers would also like to thank the following companies and picture libraries for permission to reproduce their photographs:

ALAMY IMAGES: travelstock 1.

EL BULLI RESTAURANT: 47tr.

CARDONA 7: 45clb.
CASA CALVET: 38tl.
CORBIS: Sygma/Rougemont Maurice 47tl.

DK IMAGES: Departure Lounge/Ella Milroy 11tr, 12tl/c, 15tc/crb; Departure Lounge/Paul Young 12bl, 13tr, 130br; Hiedi Grassley 19tl, 89tl, 128-9; Rough Guides/Ian Aiken 13tl/cr/br, 14cl, 15tr/bl, 75cla.

FUNDACIÓ JOAN MIRÓ: 87 all, 145cr.

GETTY IMAGES: AFPI El Bulli 27tc, 47cr; AFPI Don Emmert 17tl.

MUSEU PICASSO: © Succession Picasso/DACS 2007 14b, 81.

JEAN ORT: 6-7.

PRINCIPAL: 41bl.

RACÓ DE CAN FABES: 45bl.

TEATRE-MUSEU DALÍ: 90bl/br.

Full Page Picture Captions: Park Güell: 2; La Pedrera (Casa Mila): 8-9; Restaurant Los Caracoles: 24-5; Shop Alonso: 56-7; Shop Loft Avignon: 58-9; Palau de la Música: 72-3; El Tablao de Carmen: 92-3; República: 106-107; Sal Café 120-21; Catedral de Barcelona: 126-7; Parc de la Ciutadella: 140-41; Hotel Park: 150-51; MANC (Museu National d'Art de Catalunya): 164.

Jacket Images
Front and Spine: ALAMY IMAGES: travelstock44.de.
Back: DK IMAGES: all.